LEVELS OF THE GAME

Levels
of the Game

John McPhee

Macfarlane Walter & Ross

Toronto

First published in 1969 by Farrar, Straus & Giroux
First published by Macfarlane Walter & Ross in Canada in 1993

Macfarlane Walter & Ross
37A Hazelton Avenue
Toronto, Canada M5R 2E3

Canadian Cataloguing in Publication Data
McPhee, John, 1931–
Levels of the game
ISBN 0-921912-60-9
1. Ashe, Arthur. 2. Graebner, Clark, 1943–   .
3. Tennis—Tournaments—New York (N.Y.).
4. Tennis players—United States—Biography.
I. Title.
GV994.A7M3   1993   796.342'0922   C93-094520-4

Printed in the United States

The contents of this book originally appeared in The New Yorker *and*
were developed with the editorial counsel of William Shawn and
Robert Bingham

For Bill Bradley

LEVELS OF THE GAME

Arthur Ashe, his feet apart, his knees slightly bent, lifts a tennis ball into the air. The toss is high and forward. If the ball were allowed to drop, it would, in Ashe's words, "make a parabola and drop to the grass three feet in front of the baseline." He has practiced tossing a tennis ball just so thousands of times. But he is going to hit this one. His feet draw together. His body straightens and tilts forward far beyond the point of balance. He is falling. The force of gravity and a muscular momentum from legs to arm compound as he whips his racquet up and over the ball. He weighs a hundred and fifty-five pounds; he is six feet tall, and right-handed. His build is barely full enough not to be describable as frail, but his coördination is so extraordinary that the ball comes off his racquet at furious speed. With a step forward that stops his fall, he moves to follow.

On the other side of the net, the serve hits the grass and, taking off in a fast skid, is intercepted by the backhand of Clark Graebner. Graebner has a plan for this match. He does not intend to "hit out" much. Even if he sees the moon, he may decide not to shoot it. He will, in his words, "play the ball in the court and make Arthur play it, because Arthur blows his percentages by always trying a difficult or acute shot. Arthur sometimes tends to miss easy shots more often than he makes hard shots. The only way to get his confidence down is to get every shot into the court and let him make mistakes." Graebner, standing straight up, pulls his racquet across and then away from the ball as if he had touched something hot, and with this gesture he blocks back Ashe's serve.

Ashe has crossed no man's land and is already astride the line between the service boxes, waiting to volley. Only an extraordinarily fast human being could make a move of that distance so quickly. Graebner's return is a good one. It comes low over the net and descends toward Ashe's backhand. Ashe will not be able to hit the ball with power from down there. Having no choice, he hits it up, and weakly—but deep—to Graebner's backhand.

Graebner is mindful of his strategy: Just hit the ball in the court, Clark. Just hit the ball in the court. But Graebner happens to be as powerful as anyone who plays tennis. He is six feet two inches tall; he weighs a hundred and seventy-five pounds. The firmly structured muscles of his legs stand out in symmetrical perfection. His frame is large, but his reactions are instant and there is nothing sluggish about him. He is right-handed, and his right forearm is more than a foot in circumference. His game is built on power. His backswing is short, his strokes are compact; nonetheless, the result is explosive. There have to be exceptions to any general strategy. Surely this particular shot is a setup, a sitter, hanging there soft and helpless in the air. With a vicious backhand drive, Graebner tries to blow the ball crosscourt, past Ashe. But it goes into the net. Fifteen-love.

Graebner is nervous. He looks down at his feet sombrely. This is Forest Hills, and this is one of the semifinal matches in the first United States Open Championships. Graebner and Ashe are both Americans. The other semifinalists are a Dutchman and an Australian. It has been thirteen years since an American won the men's-singles final at Forest Hills, and this match will determine whether Ashe or Graebner is to have a chance to be the first American since Tony Trabert to win it all. Ashe and Graebner are still amateurs, and it was imagined that in this tournament, playing against professionals, they wouldn't have much of a chance. But they are here, close to the finish, playing each other. For Graebner to look across a net and see Ashe—and the reverse—is not in itself unusual. They were both born in 1943, they have known each other since they were thirteen, and they have played tournaments and exhibitions and have practiced together in so many countries and seasons that details blur. They are members of the United States Davis Cup Team and, as such, travel together throughout the year, playing for the United States—and also entering general tournaments less as individuals than en bloc, with the team.

A person's tennis game begins with his nature and background and comes out through his motor mechanisms into shot patterns and characteristics of play. If he is deliberate, he is a deliberate tennis player; and if he is flamboyant, his game probably is, too. A tight, close match unmarred by error and representative of each player's game at its highest level will be primarily a psychological struggle, particularly when the players are so familiar with each other that there can be no technical surprises. There is nothing about Ashe's game that Graebner does not know, and Ashe says that he knows Graebner's game "like a favorite tune." Ashe feels that Graebner plays the way he does because he is a middle-class white conservative. Graebner feels that Ashe plays the way he does because he is black. Ashe, at this moment, is nervous. He is famous for what journalists have called his "majestic cool," his "towering calm," his "icy elegance." But he is scared stiff, and other tennis players who know him well can see this, because it is literally true. His legs are stiff. Now, like a mechanical soldier, he walks into position to serve again. He lifts the ball, and hits it down the middle.

Ashe's principal problem in tennis has been consistency. He has brilliance to squander, but steadiness has not been characteristic of him. He shows this, woodenly hitting three volleys into the net in this first game, letting Graebner almost break him, then shooting his way out of trouble with two serves hit so hard that Graebner cannot touch them. Ashe wins the first game. Graebner shrugs and tells himself, "He really snuck out of that one."

Ashe and Graebner walk to the umpire's chair to towel off and wipe their glasses before exchanging ends of the court. Both wear untinted, black-rimmed, shatterproof glasses, and neither uses any kind of strap to hold them on. "They just stay on," Ashe will say, shoving them with his forefinger back to the bridge of his nose. Graebner's glasses have extra-long temples that curl around his ears like ram's horns. The sun is really fierce. The temperature is in the eighties. Fourteen thousand people are in the stadium. Graebner is mumbling. One of Ashe's winning serves came as a result of confusion among the officials, who delayed the action while discussing some recondite point, and, because of the delay, awarded Ashe, in accordance with the rules of the game, an extra first serve. Ashe, who seldom says much to Graebner during visits to the umpire's chair, does use the occasion now to tell Graebner that he believes the officials' decision was fair and correct. Graebner glares but says nothing. Graebner's memory for lost points and adverse calls is nothing short of perfect, and months later he will still be talking about that extra serve that turned into an ace, for he can't help thinking what an advantage he might have had if he had been able to crack Ashe open in the very first game, as he almost did anyway. Ashe, for his part, believes that it is a law of sport that everything that happens affects everything that happens thereafter, and that Graebner can simply have no idea what patterns might have followed if he had won the debated point. Having so indicated, Ashe returns to the court. It is now Graebner's turn to serve.

To the question Who has a bigger serve than Arthur Ashe?, the answer is Clark Graebner. The word most frequently used by tennis players describing Graebner's serve is "crunch": "He just tosses the ball up and crunches it." Graebner's big frame rocks backward over his right leg, then rocks forward over his left as he lifts the ball for his first serve of the match. Crunch. Ace. Right down the middle at a hundred and thirty miles an hour. Ashe is ten feet from the ball when it crosses the baseline. His racquet is only about halfway back when the ball hits the wall behind him. His face showing no expression, Ashe marches to the opposite side of the court and turns to receive the next serve. At any given moment of action, some thoughts that cross the mind of an athlete are quite conscious and others are just there, beneath the surface. Ashe will remember later on that at this particular moment in this match he is thinking, "Jesus, Graebner really hits the hell out of that first serve. He starts fast. He served nine aces in the first set against Stolle at Wimbledon, and it was over in no time." Graebner serves again—crunch, ace, right down the middle. Graebner is buoyant with sudden confidence. Ashe marches stiff-legged back across the court. The second game is Graebner's quickly. Games are one–all, first set.

Ashe lifts the ball and leans in to serve. Graebner

sways and crouches as he waits. It must have cost at least two hundred thousand dollars to produce this scene—to develop the two young men and to give them the equipment, the travel, and the experience necessary for a rise to this level. The expense has been shared by parents, sponsors, tournament committees, the Davis Cup Team, and the United States Lawn Tennis Association, and by resort hotels, sporting-goods companies, Coca-Cola, and other interested commercial supporters. The players themselves paid their way to Forest Hills for this match, though— twenty cents apiece, on the subway. Graebner lives in an apartment on East Eighty-sixth Street with his wife, Carole; their one-year-old daughter, Cameron; and their infant son, Clark. Graebner spends much of his time selling high-grade printing papers, as assistant to the president of the Hobson Miller division of Saxon Industries, and he is in love with his work. He knows the exact height and tensile strength of the corporate ladder. His boss likes tennis very much, so Graebner's present rung is the handle of a racquet. Ashe is an Army lieutenant, working in the office of the adjutant general at the United States Military Academy. He is a bachelor, and during tournament time at Forest Hills he stays at the Hotel Roosevelt. The Army is almost as tennis-minded as Graebner's boss, and Ashe has been given ample time for the game. But tennis is not, in any traditional sense, a game to him. "I get my kicks away from the tennis court," he will say. With accumulated leave time, he plans to go on safari in Kenya. It will be his first trip to Africa. In 1735, the Doddington, a square-rigger of eighty tons and Liverpool registry, sailed into the York River in Virginia carrying a cargo of a hundred and sixty-seven West African blacks. In or near York-town, the ship's captain, James Copland, traded the blacks for tobacco. One young woman, known only by a number, was acquired by Robert Blackwell, a tobacco grower from Lunenburg County. Blackwell gave her to his son as a wedding present—in the records of the county, she was listed only as "a Negur girl." According to custom, she took the name of her owner. She married a man who, having the same owner, was also named Blackwell, and they had a daughter, Lucy, whose value is given in her owner's will at fifty dollars. Lucy Blackwell married Moses Blackwell, and their daughter Peggy Blackwell had a daughter named Peggy Blackwell, who married her cousin Tony Blackwell. Their daughter Jinney mar-ried Mike, an otherwise nameless Indian of the Sauk tribe who was a blood relative of Chief Black Hawk. The preacher who married them told Mike to call himself Mike Blackwell forevermore. Jinney and Mike had a son named Hammett, who, in this chain of beings, was the last slave. Hammett was born in 1839. In 1856, he married Julia Tucker. They had twenty-three children. When he became free, he should have been given forty acres and a mule, of course, but no one gave them to him, so he bought his forty acres, in Dundas, Virginia. On the Blackwell plantation, where Hammett had lived, the plantation house—white frame, with columns—still stands, vacant and moldering. The slave cabin is there, too, its roof half peeled away. Hammett's daughter Sadie married Willie Johnson, and their daughter Amelia married Pinkney Avery Ashe. His family line reached back, in analogous fashion, to the ownership of Samuel Ashe, an early governor of the State of North Carolina, whose name, until now, has been kept alive largely by the continuing existence of Asheville. Pinkney and Amelia had a son named Arthur, who, in 1938, married Mattie Cunningham, of Richmond. Their son Arthur Junior was born in 1943.

All these names are presented on separate leaves or limbs of an enormous family tree—six by seven feet, and painted on canvas—that is kept in the home of Thelma Doswell, a cousin of Arthur Ashe. Mrs. Doswell, who lives in the District of Columbia and is a teacher of children who have specific learning disabilities, did much of the research that produced the tree, using vacation time to travel to courthouses and libraries in southern Virginia. There are fifteen hundred leaves on the tree, and one leaf—Arthur Ashe, Jr.'s—is painted gold. Matrilineal in nature, the tree was made for display at annual reunions of the family, which have been held in various cities—Washington, Bridgeport, Philadelphia, Pittsburgh—and have drawn above three hundred people. The family has a crest, in crimson, black, and gold. A central chevron in this escutcheon bears a black chain with a broken link, symbolizing the broken bonds of slavery. Below the broken chain is a black well. And in the upper corners, where the crest of a Norman family might have fleurs-de-lis, this one has tobacco leaves, in trifoliate clusters. Graebner has no idea whatever when his forebears first came to this country.

Graebner has the sun behind him now, and he means to use it. He runs around Ashe's serve, takes it on his forehand, and drives the ball up the middle. Graebner's favorite stroke is his forehand, and Ashe thinks that Graebner sometimes hits his forehands about twice as hard as he needs to, for pure Teutonic pleasure. Ashe punches back a deep volley, and Graebner throws a lob into the sun. Ashe moves back lightly, looking for the ball. In a characteristic that is pretty much his own, he prepares for overheads by pointing at the ball as it arcs down from the sky. He is like an anti-aircraft installation. Left arm up, fist closed, index finger extended, he continues to point at the ball until he has all but caught it. His racquet meanwhile dangles behind his back. Then it whips upward in the same motion as for a serve. He picks the ball out of the sun this time, but not well enough, and his shot goes into the net. Graebner plays on according to plan, forcing Ashe into another error, then finding a chance to send another lob into the sun. Ashe drops back, points, smashes—into the net. The score is now fifteen-forty. All Graebner needs is one more point to break Ashe's serve. Ashe maintains his cool appearance, but he is thinking, "My God, what's happening? Here he goes. He's going to get the first set. And if he does, my confidence is going right down the tube. Graebner is a front-runner, very tough when he's ahead. Someday he's going to get the lead on me and he's not going to give it up." In this game, Ashe's first serve has not once been successful. Perhaps enlivened by his fears, the next one goes in, hard and wide, drawing Graebner off balance, but Graebner reaches the ball and sends it low over the net and down the line. Ashe picks it up with a half volley and tries to flick it crosscourt at an acute angle, far from Graebner's reach—a fantastic shot, unbelievable. Other tennis players wonder who in his right mind would attempt something like that, but this is the way Ashe plays the game—the all but impossible shot at the tensest moment. As it happens, the shot goes out. Graebner wins the game. His strategy pays off. Ashe's serve is broken. If this were a wrestling match, Graebner could be said to have thrown his man.

Behind every tennis player there is another tennis player, and in Graebner's case the other player is his father. Clark grew up in Lakewood, Ohio, and played tennis as a boy in Lakewood Park, at Lakewood High School, and at clubs in Cleveland and Shaker Heights. Paul Graebner, Clark's father, grew up in Lakewood, and played tennis as a boy in Lakewood Park, at Lakewood High School, and at clubs in Cleveland and Shaker Heights. He was the state high-school tennis champion—a title his son would win three times. He was on the tennis team at Kenyon College and played briefly on the tournament circuit in the Middle West. He went to dental school at Western Reserve University and then went into practice with his own father, Clark's grandfather. From then until now, the major diversion of Dr. Graebner's life has continued to be tennis. His week revolves around Wednesday-afternoon and Saturday doubles games. When Clark was a beginner, however, Dr. Graebner completely gave up his own tennis for five years, and every Wednesday and Saturday and at all other practicable times he took Clark to a tennis court and patiently taught him the game. Clark was an only child, as Dr. Graebner himself had been. Clark's mother, Janet Clark Graebner, was an only child, too. Clark was seven when the formal instruction began, but he had regularly hit ground strokes with a squash racquet against a basement wall when he was three years old. Within a short time, his absolutely favorite activity was smashing tennis balls, with a proper racquet, against the door of the family garage. His mother would say to friends, "My one great big weapon over his head is 'If you don't take a nap, you can't hit the tennis ball against the garage door.'" The door happened to have windows in it, and little Clark's already Wagnerian forehand had a tendency to penetrate the glass. That was all right. Dr. Graebner covered the windows with Masonite.

When Dr. Graebner first hit strokes back and forth with Clark, they did not use a net. Dr. Graebner wanted Clark to hit a good flat stroke with follow-through, and not to worry about its altitude. When the foundation was grooved, they began to hit across a net, and to build Clark's game, shot by shot, through sheer repetition—backhands crosscourt, forehands crosscourt, forehands down the line, backhands down the line, lobs. Gradually, he just grew up into his overhead. "Every shot I hit now is built on the rudiments of my father's strokes," Clark acknowledges.

"He taught me everything. I don't think he wanted to make me a champion. He just wanted to make me as good as I wanted to be. He hit balls at me for hundreds of thousands of hours, as if he were a Ball-Boy machine."

There are in tennis any number of devices that are used as teaching aids, the Ball-Boy machine, a four-hundred-dollar mortar that belches tennis balls, being one. The Graebners used none. "I was the only device. I was the only device," Dr. Graebner says. "I wasn't trying to build a champion. I was trying to get him interested in something he could do all his life."

"We did not push Clark into tennis." (Mrs. Graebner is talking.) "It was Clark's idea. No one pushed him. He was good at baseball. He might have been a baseball player. When he was nine and ready for the Little League, his father pointed out to him that he really couldn't do both baseball and tennis, and said, 'It's your decision.' Clark said, 'There is no decision,' and he gave up baseball."

Dr. Graebner did step in unequivocally when Clark showed an interest in ice hockey. "You have too much at stake, with all that you enjoy so much, to have it stopped by someone with one blow of a hockey stick," he said.

When Clark was first learning his tennis, Dr.

Graebner in winter rented a junior-high-school gymnasium on Saturdays, and, later, took him to the indoor courts at the Cleveland Skating Club. "He hit and hit and hit," Dr. Graebner says. "He never got tired of it. You couldn't get him to stop." Dr. Graebner did what he could to keep Clark on the baseline and force him to learn ground strokes—"Get back! Get back! You're edging up again. Get back! Get your fanny around. You're not getting your hips into it"—but Clark showed considerable precocity in his desire to get to the net. Most junior players tap ground strokes at one another for four hours a match, but Graebner, even when he was ten, was playing the Big Game—going for the net, trying for the sudden kill. "From a little tyke on, he had a lot of coördination," his father says. "He had it. He was a natural."

When Dr. Graebner and Clark were not on a tennis court together, they hit badminton cocks in their back yard or played ping-pong in the basement—anything that would improve the relationship between hand and eye. Clark shot pool with his mother. Asked what the family did for vacations, Mrs. Graebner says, "Vacations? You're kidding. We went to Florida so Clark could play tennis." Lakewood is just west of Cleveland, and almost every summer afternoon in his early playing years Clark went to Lakewood Park—about eighteen acres under big elm and buckeye trees, with a bandstand, bowling greens, horseshoe pitches, and eight cement tennis courts. If his father was not with him, he played with older children, or firemen, policemen, doctors. When he was ten years old, he travelled across Cleveland to a tournament in Shaker Heights, and this was his first appearance on the East Side. A boy who lived there was Warren Danne, eleven years old at the time and so much in love with tennis that he had decided he wanted to be the best tennis player in the world. Danne would eventually be the captain of the Princeton tennis team, and in the years of early adolescence he would be the doubles partner and inseparable friend of Clark Graebner. But now, as a child, watching Clark for the first time, Warren quietly took in all the grace and power that Clark already had and decided at that moment that he was going to try to become the second-best tennis player in the world.

Graebner is now planing along through the balance of the first set, unstoppable. He hits the ball six times and wins another game. He steps aside and lets Ashe's service games go by him like fast-moving cars; then he bears down some more. Both players talk to themselves. Tennis players are forever talking to themselves, sometimes out loud, and not infrequently at a volume high enough to be heard in the upper stands.

"I should be trying something bold," Ashe says. "He's just booming his serves in there."

Graebner hits a forehand down the line. *"Get* in there," he says.

An Ashe backhand drops eight feet inside the baseline. "Don't be chicken. *Hit* the ball."

"Go *through* the ball. Don't come straight up." . . . "I don't believe it." . . . "I didn't move through that one. I was all arms on that shot." . . . "Turn your shoulder." . . . "Jesus, that was close." . . . "That's too tough." . . . "Graebner's saving himself for the next game." . . . "I've got that shot down pretty well now, that slicing backhand crosscourt." . . . "Unbelievable!" . . . "Too tough." . . . "Arthur hasn't hit a return in the court."

Graebner is almost correct. In the entire first set, Ashe returns only three of Graebner's big first serves. Points are over quickly. Only one game goes as far as deuce. The longest point played in the set consists of six shots. The average number of strokes per point is two and a half.

Ashe and Graebner play tennis with an efficiency that is thought by some to diminish tennis itself. Modern power tennis—the so-called Big Game (overwhelming serves followed by savage attacks at the net)—has now had many years in which to evolve, and Ashe and Graebner are among the ultimate re-finements of it in the United States. Statistics of tennis published half a dozen years ago gave twenty-four hundred strokes as the expectable number that would be hit by two players playing serve-and-volley tennis in a match of average length (faulted serves excluded). If a spectator closes his eyes while Ashe and Graebner are playing, he is impressed by the cumulative silence. The stretches between points are long compared to the points themselves—sudden detonations quickly over, sporadic fire on a quiet front. This match between Ashe and Graebner will be of average length, and when it is over they will have hit the ball —all faulted serves *included*—eight hundred and twenty-one times. After matches with Ashe or Graebner, some players have complained that they "didn't get enough tennis."

Reformers who remember the Old Game and think something should be done about this one have suggested eliminating the first serve or making the server serve from several feet behind the baseline. Possibly the best suggestion is that the serve be left intact—for the sheer spectacle of it—but that the server not play his next shot without first letting the ball bounce. This would tend to keep the server back near the baseline and remove the homicide from his following shot. Breaking serve would not so routinely be tantamount to breaking open a set. However, there are plenty of people who like tennis the way Ashe and Graebner play it. It is the megagame. It has the spectral charm of a Joe Louis stalking a Billy Conn in silence and then dropping him with a few echoing thuds.

Both Ashe and Graebner have a great deal of finesse in reserve behind their uncomplicated power, but it surfaces once or twice a game rather than once or twice a point. Ashe is a master of drop shots, of drop half volleys, of miscellaneous dinks and chips. He is, in the idiom of tennis, very tough at cat-and-mouse—the texture of the game in which both players, near the net, exchange light, flippy shots, acutely angled and designed for inaccessibility. Graebner is a deft volleyer, reacting quickly and dangerously at the net, but in general—although the two players technically have the same sort of game—Graebner does not have the variety of shots or the versatility that Ashe has. Ashe says that Graebner "could use a little more junk in his game."

Junk is the last thing Graebner needs at this moment. He is hitting so hard and so accurately that there is very little Ashe can do. Graebner says to himself, "Look at him. He's just slapping at my serves." Graebner is closing out the set. He is serving, and he leads five games to four and forty-fifteen. He lifts the ball. Crunch. Ace. Right down the middle. Set to Graebner. He wins the first set, six games to four. For the second time in a quarter of an hour, Ashe feels his confidence going right down the tube.

From 1946 through 1961, the United States Lawn Tennis Association's national Interscholastic Championships were held on the courts of the University of Virginia, in Charlottesville. One June day in 1949, a doctor from Lynchburg happened to be driving through Charlottesville, and when he saw all the tennis going on he stopped to watch. The high quality of the play—these were the best high-school and prep-school players in the United States—impressed him almost to the point of melancholy. Before he left, he went up to the referee of the matches and introduced himself—Robert Walter Johnson, M.D. He told the referee that he had a tennis court at home and was trying to develop some young players, and that if he could bring them over to Charlottesville sometime there would be no need to feed them or to provide rooms for them, because he would take them home after the matches each day, the distance being only sixty miles. Having said all that, Dr. Johnson asked the referee, E. T. Penzold, of Norfolk, what might be done to get the Lynchburg boys into the Charlottesville tournament.

"Fill out an application," said Penzold. "Just give me your address, and I'll send you one this winter."

Dr. Johnson had built his court in the mid-nineteen-thirties, when tennis had come to assume a priority in his mind second only to medicine. For him, this was the ultimate game in a lifetime accented with sports. He had grown up in Plymouth, North Carolina, and, as a kind of roving athlete, had gone to several universities, including Shaw, Virginia Union, and Lincoln. As a halfback at Lincoln and captain of the football team, he wore no helmet, no shoulder pads. He avoided serious injury by—in his words—"doing most of my tackling by arm." He was known as Whirlwind Johnson, and he became the highest-scoring player in the records of the Colored Intercollegiate Athletic Association. In one game, in which Lincoln was the supposed underdog, he scored forty-eight points. He took his training at Meharry Medical College. When he began his practice in Lynchburg, he was thirty-five. "I knew, from medicine, that I had built up big heart muscles and that they had to have exercise to avoid fatty infiltration. This is why athletes drop dead. I didn't want to die that way. I tried a little basketball. That didn't pan out. Then I went all out for tennis. I was self-taught. I learned by watching white players. Tennis was the hardest game to master that I had ever contacted. I was an All-American football player a couple of years, a star baseball player—but tennis I just couldn't master. I played almost every afternoon at the colored Y.M.C.A."

When the level of Dr. Johnson's game went up, he began to travel extensively to play in tournaments of the American Tennis Association, the black U.S.L.T.A. Dr. Johnson would become an important figure in the A.T.A., but in the thirties the organization was something less than cohesive and was in the hands of a group that Dr. Johnson describes as "powerful, vicious West Indians in New York." Tournaments were quite local, and Dr. Johnson and an entourage he annually assembled were among the few touring players. At times, he had two automobiles and as many as eight players in his group, and they hit all the major black tournaments—Orangeburg, Tuskegee, Charlotte, Fayetteville, Durham, Petersburg, Richmond, Baltimore, Washington, Philadelphia, Plainfield, Elizabeth, Montclair, New York. Dr. Johnson invited stars like Jimmy Sides, of Chicago, to stay with him in Lynchburg and help improve his game—and to teach Robert Walter Johnson, Jr. Harmon Fitch, of Johnson C. Smith University, the 1935 A.T.A. intercollegiate champion, lived in Lynchburg with Dr. and Mrs. Johnson the summer he won his championship, and travelled with Dr. Johnson as his doubles partner. Dr. Johnson had come to tennis too late to be a singles champion—these were the years of Reginald Weir, Nathaniel Jackson, Franklin Jackson, Lloyd Scott, Jimmy McDaniel—but his name would eventually appear on the A.T.A. Championship Roll seven times as the mixed-doubles partner of Althea Gibson, for whose development as a tennis player he was in part responsible. The tennis court he had built on his property in Lynchburg was clay at first, and was converted to *en tout cas* in 1941 by a tennis-court-building firm with headquarters on Park Avenue, in New York. Dr. Johnson held annual invitation doubles tournaments on his court, bringing in players from near and far—the District of Columbia, North Carolina, New Jersey, Michigan. He paid all expenses, and he held these tournaments throughout the nineteen-forties, finally discontinuing them because they contributed nothing to young players' development, which by 1949 was what interested him most in the game.

In the first few moments as he watched the white schoolboys in Charlottesville that day, he realized that most of them were far better tennis players than the best of the players in the men's division of the A.T.A. This not only saddened him, it challenged him. From time to time over the years, he had read sports columns in which the idea was advanced that Negro athletes lacked finesse—that they might be good runners or jumpers but could never make it in a game like tennis. This idea greatly irritated Dr. Johnson, and while he was sitting there in Charlottesville that day he could not help remembering it. That winter, an application did arrive in the mail. Dr. Johnson filled it out, and two boys from Lynchburg were entered in the national interscholastics of 1950. Nothing was said about food or shelter, but Dr. Johnson imposed his own restriction. They would go home each night to Lynchburg. Dr. Johnson wanted the tennis, and he did not want to risk losing it for any reason. As it happened, those first two entrants were going home quickly anyway. They were beaten terribly—"just unmercifully," he says when he talks about it. "They were scared to death and they were slaughtered. We were humiliated." While Dr. Johnson watched this happening, he promised himself that if it took him the rest of his life he was going to develop a young black tennis player who would play at Charlottesville and go away as the national interscholastic champion.

Before leaving, Dr. Johnson apologized to Mr. Penzold for his players' poor showing. Penzold suggested that perhaps Dr. Johnson ought to look beyond Lynchburg. Maybe he should organize a Negro national interscholastic championship—say, in May—with the idea of bringing the two finalists to Charlottesville in June. Dr. Johnson did that, in May of 1951. The number of Negro high-school tennis players that could be seined out of the American society was less than two dozen, but one of them, Willie Winn, of Wilmington, North Carolina, did achieve two early-round victories at Charlottesville before being knocked emphatically out of the tournament by Donald Dell. Dr. Johnson invited Winn and other young players to live in his house in the summer, so they could practice as a squad and travel to tournaments together. Dispassionately, he culled the unserious and the relatively unsuccessful. He engendered an *esprit* among the rest. He called them the Junior Development Team. In return for room, board, transportation, and instruction, he made them weed his garden, trim the boxwoods, clip the rosebushes, spray the apple trees. Above the techniques of the game itself, he held certain principles before them as absolute requirements —in his view—for an assault on a sport as white as tennis. Supreme among these was self-control—"no racquet throwing, no hollering, no indication of discontent with officials' calls." Since players call their own lines in the early rounds of junior tournaments, he insisted that his boys play any opponents' shots that were out of bounds by two inches or less. "We are going into a new world," he told them. "We don't want anybody to be accused of cheating. There will *be* some cheating, but we aren't going to do it." Many years later, he would say reflectively, "I wanted them to be psychologically prepared for any adversity— not to blow their cool, as they call it now, when things didn't go right."

At the Johnson table, two or three meats were served at most meals, and three or four vegetables. Candy, peanuts, popcorn, and soft drinks were forbidden at all times. If the Junior Development Team had a motto, it was "No horseplay"—the Johnson code. They learned to make their beds properly. Without fail, they hung up their clothes. When a lady came into a room, they got up, or wished they had. They learned an advanced etiquette of knives, forks, and spoons. "I want you to be accepted without being a center of attraction," he said. "I want you to be able to take care of yourself in any situation where habits or manners are important, so that you don't stand out. We are going into a new world."

Year after year, two of them went to Charlottesville, and though "slaughtered" and "humiliated" were no longer the terms for what generally happened to them, none got particularly far. Meanwhile, Dr. Johnson got a call one day in 1953 from Ronald

Charity, a recent graduate of Virginia Union, in Richmond, and a ranking player in the men's division of the A.T.A. Charity said he had been working part time teaching tennis in a public park, and for several seasons he had been hitting the ball with a small boy whose physique was not prepossessing but who hit the ball well and seemed to care a great deal about playing tennis. Charity hoped that although the boy was only ten years old the doctor would let him come to Lynchburg. Dr. Johnson said, "All right, Ronald. I'll take him for a while, if you want to carry him up here." Charity drove to Lynchburg on a Sunday, and introduced Dr. Johnson to Arthur Ashe, Jr. The doctor's eyes narrowed when he saw him, and he wondered if the child had been a victim of rickets, he was so bony and frail. Arthur hit a few tennis balls, and Dr. Johnson, watching him run, was afraid he would pitch forward and fall.

Graebner waits for Ashe to hit the first serve of the second set. Ashe, in fifteen years, has filled out and has become a trim arrangement of sinews. He is lithe and springy, and his bearing is the bearing of a complete athlete—reactions twice as fast as the imagination, motions graceful and decisive, in balance, under control. Graebner is less believable. He could be a lifeguard, or an ad for a correspondence course in muscle development. Ashe has small ears, a narrow, foxlike face, short hair, and a nose so thin and straight that some Negroes say it is Ashe's nose that makes him acceptable to whites. His glasses make him look scholarly, which he is not, although he could be. He seems closer to it than most tennis players. His skin is light, but during the summer in the sun it gets darker and darker, and by the time of Forest Hills it is practically black. "I get very tan," he explains. His voice cracks with youthful throatiness. When he takes off his glasses, the rims of his eyes are light. When he takes off his wristwatch or his sweatbands, the skin that was beneath them is much lighter than that which surrounds it. Graebner, for his part, sincerely wishes that he could play with his shirt off. He is aggressively vain about his tan. "After we played in San Juan two years ago, I was as dark as Arthur," he says proudly. When he is sunbathing, he will snap at anyone who stands between him and direct sunlight for as much as three seconds. Discounting his natural advantage, Ashe tans better than Graebner does. Graebner has thick, dark hair and a facial bone structure that suggests heroic possibilities. He appears to have been cut out of a Sunday newspaper, for he looks exactly like—that is to say, he bears something far more precise than a striking resemblance to—Clark Kent, the mild-mannered reporter who has occasionally been mistaken for a bird before being positively identified as Superman. "Clark Graebner looks like Clark Kent and he knows it" is a sentence that has been uttered by more than one American tennis player now playing on the world-class, or Graebner, level. Graebner's nickname in tennis is Superboy. A few people refer to him as Herr Graebner, for he has the posture and the presence of a first lieutenant in the Wehrmacht—absolutely perpendicular when he walks, his arms swinging, a goose step suggested but not quite executed. His general gait has been widely interpreted as a swagger, particularly at moments like this one, with the applause for his performance in the first set still sounding in the air.

Ashe is remembering one of the precepts of Dr. Johnson, who is watching all this from a preferred position—a seat high in the northeast corner of the stadium. Dr. Johnson is seventy now. His hairline has receded and the hair beyond it is swept back. His frame retains the form of a football halfback. Dr. Johnson always told the Junior Development Team that the first point played in any set was of considerable psychological importance. A perceptible edge can go to the winner of that point. As the case may be, that one point can restore, maintain, deflate, or destroy confidence. Confidence goes back and forth across a tennis net much like the ball itself, and only somewhat less frequently. If two players are on about the same level, no matter what that level is, the player who experiences more minutes of confidence will be the winner. Frequently enough, Graebner has heard Ashe quote Dr. Johnson on the importance of the first point in a set. Graebner knows that Ashe wants this one, and Graebner wants it, too. He wipes his right hand on a towel that always sticks out of his pocket. The towel is the sort that is clipped around the necks of his father's patients ("Open wide, please"). Graebner further dries his hand by blowing on it, and, finally, by rubbing it over the gut of his racquet. Ashe goes up to hit the ball. It is a big serve. Graebner blocks it back. Ashe, trying to pick the ball up with a running half volley, sends it into the net. Love-fifteen.

Ashe is consciously scared. In nervous situations in the past, he has been attacked by stomach cramps that doubled him over. In Davis Cup competition, while Graebner is playing singles, Ashe sometimes gets so nervous that he leaves the scene and listens to the match on the radio. Graebner strides into position. Ashe wins the next point, and the next. Graebner ties the game at thirty-all. Ashe hits a flat serve too deep. Then he spins a second one in. Graebner runs around it and smashes a forehand up the center. Ashe takes it at the service line and, without bending down, flips an underhand volley to Graebner at the baseline. Graebner, on his heels and off balance, hits a powerful backhand at Ashe, who punches a volley deep to the backhand corner. Graebner runs, sets, and hits the ball down the line. Ashe handles it badly, and the point—the longest so far—is over. The score is thirty-forty. This could be the match, right here. If Graebner wins the next point, breaking Ashe, Ashe may very well not recover.

Graebner dries his hand on the gut. Graebner's hand has two big calluses on it—one just below the little finger, and the other on the butt of the palm. These act more or less as an oarlock for his racquet handle as he shifts his grip for a forehand or a backhand. Graebner is thinking, "If I break him now, his morale has had it."

Ashe spins his racquet and looks inscrutable. Ashe has a single, enormous callus—a half inch thick— just below his index finger. No matter what stroke he may be hitting, he never changes his grip. He is saying to himself, "This could be serious, Arthur. What's *happening*? One little mistake here and it's curtains. You want to play chicken, but you have to fight it. *Hit* the ball." His serve goes down the middle, to Graebner's forehand side. Graebner swings late and slices the ball across the net at a sharp angle.

If it drops in, Ashe cannot possibly get to it. The ball lands one inch out.

On a flood of relief, Ashe jerks Graebner around the court in two commanding points, hitting bullet volleys and a loose, almost mocking drop shot. He now leads, one game to love, second set.

Graebner serves, and Ashe pounds the ball back at him in a way that reminds Graebner that Ashe can not only put down a threat but make one as well. Graebner slugs the ball, and Ashe slugs it back. The reports are loud. Ashe and Graebner are really hitting. Each is advertising his power. Neither is aiming for the corners. They are shooting right at each other. Graebner creams another one, but Ashe's mood changes and he throws up a light, soft lob into the sun. Blinding rays hit Graebner just before Graebner hits the ball, into the net.

"People say that Arthur lacks the killer instinct." (Ronald Charity is commenting.) "And that is a lot of baloney. Arthur is quietly aggressive—more aggressive than people give him credit for being. You don't get to be that good without a will to win. He'll let you win the first two sets, then he'll blast you off the court." Ronald Charity, who taught Arthur Ashe to play tennis, was himself taught by no one. "I was my own protégé," he says. Charity is approaching forty and is the head of an advertising and public-relations firm in Danville, Virginia. Trim, lithe, in excellent condition, he is still nationally ranked as one of the top ten players in the A.T.A. In 1946, when he began to play tennis, as a seventeen-year-old in Richmond, there were—male and female, all ages— about twenty Negroes in the city who played the game, and none of them played it well. Charity, as a college freshman, thought tennis looked interesting, and when, in a bookstore, he saw Lloyd Budge's "Tennis Made Easy" he bought a copy and began to teach himself to play. When he had absorbed what Budge had to say, he bought Alice Marble's "The Road to Wimbledon," and, finally, William T. Tilden's "How to Play Better Tennis." "It just happened that I could pull off a page and project into my imagination how it should be done," he says. Blacks in Richmond could play tennis at the Negro Y.W.C.A., where Charity developed his game, and, a little later, four hard-surface courts were built at Brook Field, a Negro playground about two miles from the heart of the city. Arthur Ashe, a Special Police Officer in charge of discipline at several Negro playgrounds, lived in a frame house in the middle of Brook Field. When Arthur Ashe, Jr., was six years old, he spent a great deal of time watching Ronald Charity play tennis, and would never forget what he felt as he watched him: "I thought he was the best in the world. He had long, fluid, graceful strokes. I could see no kinks in his game."

"I guess by that time I was about the best in Richmond—you know, black tennis player," Charity continues. "One day, Arthur asked me if I would show him how to play. He had had no tennis experience. I put the racquet in his hand. I taught him the Continental grip. That's what I was playing with. At first, I would stand six feet away from him, on the same side of the net, and throw balls to him while he learned a stroke. The little guy caught on so quickly. When the stroke had been taught, I would cross the net and hit it with him. We practiced crosscourt forehands, forehands down the line, crosscourt backhands. We played every summer evening. There was a little backboard there. All day long, he would practice. We had a club—the Richmond Racquet Club, all grown men—and we let him join it. His game improved. One day, when he was playing someone his own age, he kept looking around after he hit good shots, to see who might have been watching. I bawled him out for it. I told him if he continued to do anything like that I wasn't going to be bothered with him anymore. He never did that anymore. He was a quiet child, observant. He took in everything, and read a lot. He was very disciplined. The level of his game kept going up. Finally, I called Dr. Johnson at Lynchburg. In fact, I carried Arthur up there. It was on a Sunday. He was ten years old."

Dr. Johnson's house, two stories, frame, painted brown and white, is about twice the size of any other house in the neighborhood. It has four upstairs bedrooms, one of which Arthur shared with another boy. The basement playroom appears to be a copy of a small night club on a busy highway. The columns that support the floor above are encased in blue mirrors. Red leatherette couches and lounge chairs are set about in groups. Glass doors, which are generally locked, close off a bar that is commercial in grandeur and is fully appointed and equipped. Tennis trophies shine from every shelf. There is a pingpong table, for hand-eye coördination. Off the lounge is a shower room. A basement door and stairwell lead to a formal garden, and across the garden is the tennis court, surrounded by a rusting fence and high telephone poles that support floodlights. The tennis court abuts the sidewalk that runs in front of the doctor's house, and is several feet above the sidewalk level, held there by a retaining wall of poured concrete. People walking by have a sneaker's-eye view of the action. On the other side of Pierce Street is a small general store, and next to the store are two narrow, vacant houses that have no doors and few windowpanes. Boards nailed on a slant across the doors carry boldly lettered but apparently ineffectual warnings against vandalism and trespass. Behind Dr. Johnson's house is a combined garage and tool shed that contains a curious device. From a bracket on the floor to a beam above runs a vertical elastic cord, drawn fairly taut. About two feet off the floor, the cord passes through the center of a tennis ball. The height of the ball is adjustable. The developing tennis players hit this ball with pieces of broom handle cut twenty-six inches long, the exact length of a tennis racquet. The device, known as the Tom Stow Stroke Developer, was invented by the teacher of Sarah Palfrey, Helen Jacobs, Margaret Osborne, and J. Donald Budge. Dr. Johnson has almost every teaching device known to the game. On the court are two Ball-Boy machines, a rebounding net, and a service stand, which holds a ball in perfect position overhead for practicing serves. Players who are new to the Junior Development Team swing broom handles at the Tom Stow Stroke Developer until they can connect consistently with the ball and not the cord. Then they take their broom handles to the court and use them instead of racquets. Dr. Johnson calls this "learning how to *see* the ball." When they can play proficiently with the broom handles, actually rallying, they are advanced to the use of strung frames.

The Junior Development Team has generally had eight or ten members. In recent summers, white boys have applied for admission, and Dr. Johnson has let some in. Dr. Johnson's effect on his neighborhood has been analogous to his effect on the outside world. In the living room of his next-door neighbor's house, a small, one-story place on the far side of the tennis court, is a table on which are twenty-nine tennis trophies. Near the table is a television set. Two teen-age boys, the winners of the trophies, are watching Ashe and Graebner, at Forest Hills, on television. Graebner hits a serve that splits the court, landing on the line between the service boxes and almost instantly thereafter smashing into the stadium wall. Ashe does not even lift his racquet. He is not bothered by an ace that is perfect. "If the ball goes right on the line in the center, there is nothing you can do," he will say. "There is something in your mind that says you can't get there." The score is fifteen-all, second game, second set. One of the boys watching television sighs audibly through his teeth: "Shhhhh . . ."

When Arthur first saw Dr. Johnson's place, it looked much as it does now. The houses across the street were occupied then. The fence around the court was less rusty. There was no night lighting. But the training gadgets were there, and a group of high-school boys were intently learning not only how to play but, more important, how to win. "My ambition was to develop somebody who could win the U.S.L.T.A. Interscholastic Championship—that was it, pure and simple," Dr. Johnson says. "I had so many players right on the verge. Then they would fall off." When Arthur had been there less than three days, Dr. Johnson decided he was unteachable, and told him he was going to send him home. Arthur's trouble was that he responded to the Johnson method by telling Dr. Johnson—and Dr. Johnson's son Robert, who did a lot of the teaching—how Ronald Charity would have done things, with the implication that Ronald Charity knew more than they did. Dr. Johnson called Arthur Ashe, in Richmond, and suggested that he come and get his son. Among the talents of Arthur Senior, the discipline of children was not the least. Once, at Brook Field, when Arthur Junior threw his racquet in exasperation, he heard the screen door of his house slam before the racquet hit the ground. His father was on the tennis court three seconds later, and Arthur Ashe, Jr., has not to this day flung a racquet in anger again. Now Arthur Senior drove straightaway to Lynchburg, stepped onto Dr. Johnson's tennis court, and asked his son if he wanted to stay with Dr. Johnson. When Arthur Junior said he did, his father said, "Then you do everything he says, no matter what he tells you."

Assuring Dr. Johnson that the problem no longer existed, Arthur Senior left Lynchburg. Dr. Johnson would always thereafter praise Arthur Ashe as the most unquestioningly obedient tennis player he had ever coached. If Dr. Johnson told Arthur to hit to an opponent's backhand and nowhere else, Arthur would hit to the backhand even if the other player edged over so far that ninety per cent of the court was on his forehand side. "Whatever strategy you gave him to play, he wouldn't change to save his life," Dr. Johnson says. "He did what you told him, even if he lost at it."

Training time was divided among the players, and Arthur, lowest in age and seniority, had to spend a lot of time standing around watching the older boys play, much as Rodney Laver, a few years earlier, had spent a lot of time standing around the tennis court on his family's farm in tropical Australia waiting for his older brothers to finish playing. The boys in Lynchburg would take turns hitting against a Ball-Boy until they missed, or until they had hit a hundred times—always concentrating on one stroke until they had it under control. They rarely played points. "I believe in practice," Dr. Johnson told them. "You can learn more." There was one boy there near Arthur's age level. His name was Horace Cunningham. He lived just across the street from Dr. Johnson, and, as the Doctor continues the story, "He could beat Arthur's socks off. Arthur was the worst player. He was always the last one to leave the court—that was one thing in his favor. But everybody could beat him."

In Arthur's eyes, the Doctor was an imperial figure —"an immensely rich Negro, with his tennis court and his Buick, and his seemingly endless supply of money. At ten and eleven years old, I was always rather awed by the guy. The world is very small then. To tell you the truth, I hated everything about Dr. Johnson's at that time, except playing tennis. I hated weeding the gardens, cleaning the doghouse. I was the youngest, and I had to clean the doghouse every day."

Dr. Johnson to this day takes visitors out back, shows them the concrete-floored pen where he keeps his hunting dogs, and demonstrates how easy the enclosure is to clean. "All he had to do was use a water hose," he says. "Some kids are lazy. The least they can do is to weed the garden, roll the court, clean the doghouse—when I am paying for their room and board. Arthur's trying to have some fun, griping about that." Standing there with the hose in his hand, Dr. Johnson looks away toward the tennis court and forgets all about the dog pen. "Even when Arthur started going off to play in the tournaments, Horace could beat him—on this court. But Horace could *not* beat Arthur in the tournaments. That was a different situation." They travelled in the Buick—Baltimore, Washington, Durham—and when Arthur was a little older and began to go to some tournaments on his own, Dr. Johnson called him, wherever he might be, to talk over his matches. Arthur was based in Lynchburg every summer until he was eighteen, the fixed element in a squad whose personnel changed frequently, as Dr. Johnson did his own kind of weeding. The Junior Development Team functioned in part on contributions from interested people in the A.T.A., but Dr. Johnson put thousands of dollars of his own specifically into Arthur's career. Three white businessmen in Richmond—an insurance broker, a department-store executive, and a legitimate-theatre executive—contributed significant amounts, and Arthur's father gave more than he could afford. Arthur once overheard him saying that he was a little sorry his son had chosen a sport as expensive as tennis. The cost of equipment alone was more than a thousand dollars a year.

When Arthur was fifteen, Dr. Johnson tried to enter him in the junior tournament of the Middle Atlantic Lawn Tennis Association, which was held at the Country Club of Virginia, in Richmond. The Middle Atlantic L.T.A., a semi-autonomous subdivision of the U.S.L.T.A., refused to process the application. So Arthur could earn no ranking among boys in his home section of the country, although by now he was ranked fifth among boys in the United States. The following summer, 1959, the Middle Atlantic Championships were held at the Congressional Country Club in Bethesda, Maryland, and Arthur's application arrived "too late." In 1960, Arthur won the junior championship of the A.T.A. *and* the A.T.A. men's-singles championship. He was seventeen. He has sometimes been compared, in his sport, to Jackie Robinson in baseball, but the analogy is weak and foreshortens the story. Jackie Robinson was part of a pool of many hundreds of first-rate baseball players, and was chosen from among them to cross the color line. Arthur, at the age of seventeen, had beaten and far outdistanced all the Ronald Charitys there were. Already he stood, as he has remained, alone. Even at that time there was not one Negro in the United States who could effectively play tennis with him, and there is none now. In June, 1961, he went to Charlottesville in the Buick with Dr. Johnson, and he won the U.S.L.T.A. national Interscholastic Championship without losing a set. He remembers what he thought at that moment in his life: "I saw that it was conceivable that I might win someday at Forest Hills."

In 1962, the Interscholastic Championships, which

had been held in Charlottesville for sixteen consecutive years, were moved to Williamstown, Massachusetts.

Ashe wants to level things. He is uncomfortable looking uphill at Graebner, who hits another serve of almost unplayable force but just close enough to be reached. Ashe dives for it and stops it with his racquet. His return floats across the net and drops near the sideline. Graebner has difficulty believing that the ball has come back. He is not reacting. "Unbelievable," he says to himself. "Too tough." After this momentary lapse, he sprints for the ball, and is completely off the court when he gets to it. Despite Graebner's hesitation, and despite the inconvenient location of Ashe's shot, Graebner has reached the ball in time not only to hit it but to drive it. Many players think Graebner is slow, for somehow, to an athlete's eye, he looks slow, and they will say something like "From the waist up, Graebner is the fastest in the world, but his feet are in his way." Ashe does not wholly agree. "Graebner is mechanically fast," he will say. "He's not that agile. He can't reverse directions well, but once he gets rolling in one direction he is fast. You've got to finesse Graebner. He's as strong as an ox. Get the ball anywhere within a two-step radius of his body and you're dead. You can't go through him. You've got to go around him or over him." Graebner says, "I don't look fast, but I get to the ball."

Graebner's drive is deep to Ashe's backhand corner, and Ashe intercepts it with a beautiful, fluid crosscourt stroke. In the follow-through, he is up on his toes, arms flaring. Ashe's backhand is one of the touchstones of modern tennis. Graebner is disturbed. He is thinking, "There it is. There Arthur goes, swinging freely." Arthur swinging freely is something that scares players of all nations. When he is behind, or otherwise in trouble, he reacts by hitting all the harder, going for a winner on every ball. Graebner moves to cover the shot. Graebner may not be technically agile, but he is moving like a cat right now. Ashe is a little surprised, and thinks, "Good God! Clark is covering that net like a blanket." Graebner gets the ball with a lunging backhand volley, his shoes slip on the grass, and he breaks his fall with his left arm. The volley is deep. Ashe detonates another splendid backhand, down the line. But Graebner recovers his balance and stops the ball at the net, dinking a shot that Ashe, sprinting, cannot reach. "What a greasy shot!" Ashe says to himself. "Gee, that pisses me off. He just greased it. I hit two great shots, then he greased one. It barely got over the net, and it died in the grass."

Now, for the first time in the match, Graebner double-faults. He scowls angrily toward the Marquee, the sheltered stands at the eastern end of the stadium, where his wife, Carole, is sitting with Ashe's father and Robert J. Kelleher, president of the U.S.L.T.A. Carole is the trim in Graebner's racquet—the extra bit of nylon stringing that determines rough or smooth. Graebner's angry look seems to say that he believes it was Carole who served the double fault. She absorbs this, by grace and by agreement. "I tell him to look over at me when he gets mad, because I would rather have him get mad at me than at anyone else—or at himself," she explains. For one reason or another—not always anger—Graebner looks at Carole about a hundred times a match. "I try to give him an opportunity to meet my eyes after each point, if he wants to," she goes on. "If he needs a little pick-me-up, I am there." If she is not there, he may fall apart. Once, in Australia, in a tight moment, he looked for Carole and she had gone off momentarily for refreshments. "Where's Carole? Where's Carole?" he said, and he ran around behind the grandstand looking for her. Now, at Forest Hills, she raises one hand and makes a patting motion, as if she were soothing an invisible horse. This signal means "Calm down." If she raises two clenched fists, it means "Come on, now. Get your second wind. This is a big point." If she puts one hand on top of her head and shakes her head, it means "Unbelievable!"—or, in translation, "Good shot." Graebner responds to these messages in part because his wife, whose maiden name was Carole Caldwell, is a world-class tennis player. She is ranked sixth among women players in the United States. She plays very little now, but she has been ranked as high as fourth in the world, and might be there still if she did not have two children under two years of age. "I think these are the only times that Clark publicly acknowledges me as a knowing player," she says. "Off the court, he does not acknowledge that I know much about the game. I live my tennis through Clark now, so I don't miss it so much. During matches, I'm perfectly frank with him. If he's not playing well, I'll let him know. I think he could be the best there is. Up to now, I don't think he has really worked at it. He is a natural player, not a made player. I think he sometimes thinks, 'Oh, what the hell. If God didn't give it to me, why go after it?' He sometimes loses faith in himself. As soon as he starts to lose, or get depressed, his shoulders drop. I don't think Clark would admit this, but in some respects I am his self-confidence. He will not admit that he is the biggest baby in the world, and he is by far. You wouldn't exactly call him docile. If he makes a great point, I clap hard. He'll turn and smile sometimes." At Forest Hills in 1965, Carole and Clark won the national husband-and-wife doubles championship, and she says she will never enter it again, because they fought constantly and Clark complained that she wouldn't do what he told her to do. "I've won a lot of tournaments. Let me play my own game," she said to him. A few minutes later, Clark told her to lob, so she hit the ball down the line. Even recreationally, they almost never play together now, except when Clark has not played for a long time and wants to regroove. Men frequently hit with women to regroove their strokes. Carole is a good-looking blue-eyed brunette, attractively selfless, gifted with discipline, constantly starving herself to control the figure that gave her the big tennis game that made her fourth in the world. She grew up in Santa Monica. She has girlish animation, and, blushing through it, she discloses that she was named "for Carole Lombard, who was married to Clark Gable."

Ashe is thinking, "Graebner just looked at his wife." And behind Arthur's impassive face—behind the enigmatic glasses, the lifted chin, the first-mate-on-the-bridge look—there seems to be a smile. Progress against Graebner in any given match, many players believe, can be measured directly by the number of times Graebner has looked at his wife.

Ashe tries to pass Graebner, and hits the ball into

the net a foot and a half below the tape. Graebner has him forty-thirty. Ashe looks within himself angrily, thinking, "You choked on that one, boy."

As Graebner gets ready to serve for the game, Ashe tells himself, "You . . . better . . . be . . . tough . . . now."

Crunch. Ashe flails and misses. "Fault!" cries Frank Hammond, who is the service linesman on the side of the court where Ashe is at the moment playing. There are thirteen officials around the court, and Ashe and Graebner know them all. Frank Hammond's job is particularly sensitive—watching the service line in a match between two players whose styles revolve around their ballistic serves. Both Ashe and Graebner specifically asked for Hammond today, in part because they like him, and in part because they consider him the best service linesman at Forest Hills. Unconsciously, they may also feel drawn to Hammond because he is—literally—Santa Claus on a grand scale. He is a large, jolly man of national reputation, who, purely for his own amusement, is an itinerant Santa Claus, appearing in a different city each Christmas season. This year, he plans to be at Lord & Taylor, in New York. Ashe mumbles, "Good call, Frank." Ashe is still alive in this game, thanks to Santa Claus's photoelectric eyes. The serve was a half inch long.

Graebner's second serve curves in. Ashe meets it with a graceful, underspinning backhand. Graebner leans forward to volley from his shoetops. The ball is floating before Ashe now. Graebner is at the net, astride the center line, perfectly balanced and ready, but he has given Ashe too much time. Ashe hits another backhand—a hard, rolling, top-spin backhand, with unimprovable placement. It slants past Graebner so fast he can take only one step in its direction, and it skips through the chalk of the sideline—a duster, as players call a shot that stirs the chalk. For the first time in the match, Ashe has forced Graebner, serving, to deuce. "Oh, God! His play will pick up from here," thinks Graebner, who has read this sort of tea leaf before. Ashe's great shot does not necessarily mean that others will immediately follow, but it reminds Graebner of what can emerge, suddenly, from beneath the general surface of play. Moments later, Graebner, moving with extraordinary anticipation, picks off a forehand drive and, with an adroit, slicing drop shot off his steel racquet, puts the ball away. "I actually have more touch with the steel than anyone else," Graebner will say. "Graebner grips the racquet so tight he can *feel* the ball," Ashe observes. "He must get writer's cramp."

Advantage Graebner. Crunch. The serve is too

much—unplayable. Game to Graebner. Games are one–all, second set.

The match, for a time, becomes a simple exhibition of the service stroke. Ashe may not have quite Graebner's power, but his serves—in the vernacular of the game—move better than Graebner's do. They follow less predictable patterns, and they come off the grass in less expectable ways. "I can feel my serve from my toes to my fingertips," he will say. "I don't have to look. It just flows." In two games against Ashe's service, the only point Graebner wins is given to him in the form of a double fault. This, to Arthur Ashe, Sr., is a sign of impatience on the part of his son. He says, "When Arthur Junior rushes himself, he gets into trouble." Mr. Ashe is an axiomatic man. When he says things like that, he does not seem to be making a comment so much as he seems to be promulgating a law of the universe. Somewhat darker than Arthur Junior, he is just under six feet tall and has a small mustache and a full, round face. He wears bifocal glasses with black metal rims. He is a disciplinarian by profession, and he has a kind of stern, forthright self-assurance that is not put on for the job. In several ways, he differs notably from his son. Arthur Junior is particularly articulate, and Mr. Ashe is not particularly articulate. His education stopped when he was eleven years old. Arthur Junior's personality is contained, controlled, withheld. In Arthur Senior there is no studied cool. His smile is quick. He jokes a lot. He is easy to know.

For some years now, he has lived in the country near Gum Spring, thirty-five miles northwest of Richmond. He gets up at five-thirty in the morning. ("If I stay in bed after five-thirty, I get mischievous.") He drives into Richmond in a white Ford pickup that has an aluminum enclosure behind the cab and contains a chain saw and dozens of other tools, which equip him for his three jobs and his various categories of responsibility. He wears, typically, a red shirt, gray cotton trousers, a gray cap. A bunch of keys hangs from one hip. He has his own landscaping business and his own janitorial business, and he seems to specialize in medical centers, banks, and office buildings in the new industrial parks of Richmond's west end. "You've got to scramble," he says. "You've got to give from one hand to gain on the other." He has eight employees. Some of them irritate him by following customs that run counter to his axioms—for example, when he gives them eighty dollars' pay on a Friday and they borrow two dollars from him on Monday. From 2 P.M. until 10 P.M. each day, he works for the city. In the Department of Recreation and Parks, he is not only a Special Police

Officer but also a pool engineer and the supervisor of tennis courts. He carries a nightstick, handcuffs, and a gun, but he wears no uniform. His primary duty is to maintain order, and he doesn't seem to mind that his work has made him from time to time unpopular. Humor spills out of him wherever he goes. He goes into a hardware store during the hunting season and asks for a three-gun rack for his car. The salesman says, "Why do you need a *three*-gun rack, Arthur?" and the answer is "You always need a third gun so you can shoot your wife."

Mr. Ashe has five houses—four in Richmond and the one in Gum Spring—and he says that he maintains all these dwellings less for the rents than as a form of self-protection. "I'm like a groundhog. Shoot at him and he has another home to scurry off to." He built his house in Gum Spring with his own hands, using materials that he salvaged from houses and other buildings that were razed when Interstate 95 cleaved Richmond some years ago. His property is isolated among cornfields and woods of oak and pine on a narrow asphalt road. The house is one-story, thirty-six by forty-six feet, with walls of cement block painted aquamarine. Mr. Ashe is an adept carpenter, plumber, electrician, and mason, and for a number of years he regularly took Arthur Junior to Gum Spring to work on the new house.

"Arthur Junior toted boards, mixed mortar, pulled nails, helped set the block. He did any damned thing I told him to do."

"Daddy is a Jack-of-all-trades, but that's not my bag. I hated it, but I never let him know. We went out every weekend. I had no choice."

"You give from one hand to gain on the other."

The living room at Gum Spring is full of tennis plaques and trophies, won by Arthur and his brother John, who is five years younger. On one wall hang a copy of the Twenty-third Psalm stamped in brass and a portrait of Christ painted on a china plate. Above the psalm and the plate is the head of an eight-point stag. "The first time Arthur Junior went deer hunting was in King William County." (His father gets inordinate pleasure from telling this story.) "He was just a boy. I put him on a stump and told him to wait for deer. He was nervous, just like his mother. He's got over it now, but he was nervous. And *seven* deer came toward him, and he shouted, 'Daddy! Daddy! Daddy!' I shouted, 'Shoot that damn gun.' He killed two." The house is heated with wood fires, and the stove in the kitchen is also fuelled with wood. In every room is the scent of burning oak. As Mr. Ashe drives around the countryside near Gum Spring, he turns into a fanatic for neatness and tidiness, and gets visibly angry at the sight of houses surrounded by automobile parts, miscellaneous cordwood, old oil drums, piles of scrap lumber. He says that people have no right to mess up the landscape that way. Then he drives into his own property, which is bestrewn with automobile parts, miscellaneous cordwood, oil drums, scrap lumber, and gravel, and he explains that things are different here, because he knows exactly what and where everything is and the use to which he intends to put it.

There are six in the family. Arthur Junior and John have a stepsister, Loretta, and a stepbrother, Robert. Soon after John was born, his mother (and Arthur's) died. Several years later, Mr. Ashe married Lorraine Kimbrugh, a practical, witty, conversational woman, who frequently keeps Arthur up until two or three in the morning talking about his travels and the worlds he plays in. Robert and Loretta are in high school. John is a Marine sergeant, recently home from Vietnam. More solid in build than his older brother, he is an excellent general athlete, but not a specialist. In high school in Richmond, he won letters in football, basketball, baseball, track, and tennis. Nonetheless, in finding his own way he is inevitably encountering the inconvenience of being so closely related to Arthur Ashe. A football scholarship is open to him at Duke, but he is thinking of staying in the Marine Corps.

Some people have criticized Mr. Ashe for "hustling" lumber to build the Gum Spring house. "It's against their pride," he explains. "But they have notes on their houses, and I don't." He still makes regular calls at the Richmond city dump to look for scrap lumber and other materials. He has built a large combined garage and tool shed using heavy-gauge tin highway signs—"Fredericksburg 25," "Williamsburg 99"—as siding. In this building is a twenty-one-foot aluminum-hulled power boat with a 100-horsepower engine. With his family, he cruises and fishes the rivers and tidewaters of Virginia. Arthur Junior is never reluctant to go on these trips, for fishing is his bag, too.

Graebner serves the fourth game of the second set, and in the entire game there are eight shots. Two are misfired serves. Two are aces. Ashe gets his racquet on the ball only twice. Dr. Graebner, on the edge of his chair, is pleased. "He's taking his time. He's reading Arthur nicely. He's hitting well." As it happens, Dr. Graebner is not at Forest Hills but at his home, on Wimbledon Road, in Beachwood, Ohio, where, with Clark's mother, he is watching the match on a television screen that seems almost as large as the huge picture window behind it. Through the window is an awning-shaded terrace, and beyond that a compact lawn. "I just wish he'd learn to smile on the court, because he looks so grim, and he just isn't," Mrs. Graebner says. When Clark moves with correct anticipation to cover a shot, Dr. Graebner says, "He read that well." The houses of Wimbledon Road appear to be in the fifty-to-seventy-thousand-dollar class and almost too big for the parcels of land allotted to them. They are faced with stratified rock, lightened with big windows, surrounded with shrubbery, and lined up in propinquous ranks like yachts at a pier. Arthur Ashe has visited the Graebners' house several times, and he remembers it in blueprint detail. "You walk in the front door. You face steps. The dining room is on the left-hand side. The living room is on the right, and beyond it a den. Beyond the dining room, the kitchen. Big back yard. Four bedrooms." The Graebners' living-room shelves are filled with tennis trophies, in place of books. The room has big furniture—big couches, big easy chairs, big lamps, big coffee tables. Mrs. Graebner is a large woman with a strikingly attractive face, curiously like Carole's, and she, too, is a dieter of fearful discipline. Dr. Graebner is extremely dental. He has bright-white, flawless teeth—a kind of self-portrait—in an open face that smiles readily. He speaks quickly and nervously, often in an engaging monologue. Tennis players who visit his home uniformly like him, and find him amusing because he asks them questions

("How are you? How was your trip? How is your game?") and, not waiting for replies, answers all the questions himself ("It's nice to see you so well. There's nothing like a good, smooth flight. You're having your best year"). Attentively, he worries over his guests. "That's all right. We'll get a towel. It will be O.K. All right. There will be no difficulty," he says, and he all but concludes by saying, "Relax, now. It won't hurt a bit." After thirty years of close contact with temporarily muted people, he has mastered the histrionisms of his craft. He winks, interviews himself, speaks always reassuringly, and couples his skeins of language with "but"s and "and"s, never stopping. Crunch. Ace. Right down the middle. "He's taking his time. He's hitting well." Dr. Graebner is almost completely absorbed in Clark—in everything from the mechanical functioning of his game to the general politics of tennis, which can take on cinquecento overtones when powers meet to set up a tournament draw—and many of Dr. Graebner's long-standing, old-Clevelander patients have learned that the last thing they want to say as they sit down in the chair is "How's Clark?"

Dr. Graebner's hair, crew cut, is speckled salt-and-pepper gray, but he looks so much like Clark that the two could be mistaken for brothers. He is just over six feet tall. Like Clark, Dr. Graebner has a quick, hot temper. "My father and I are very similar. He is tight, keyed up, a perfectionist, a hard worker. He does orthodonture—everything but surgery. He's a nervous person, I guess. So am I. We keep a lot inside ourselves. He doesn't drink, smoke, or swear. I don't do anything to an extreme, but I am not a puritanical soul."

"My father can barely read and write. In his own simple way, though, he is very broadminded. He is receptive to new ideas. He shows little concern for social conventions. He is a benevolent man. He gives money and clothes to the poor. He was always strict, but fair. He doesn't drink. So far as I know, he has never bought a bottle of liquor. We do have homemade wine—peach wine, blackberry wine. If my father had a million dollars, he wouldn't change. He is not by any means a social climber. I'm convinced of that." Mr. Ashe was born on a farm in South Hill, Virginia. He had eight brothers and sisters. His father, Pink Ashe, was a carpenter-bricklayer-farmer who grew tobacco and corn. When Arthur Senior was twelve, he went to Richmond to make his living, but he had been working part time almost all his life—cleaning yards, carrying wood, cleaning chicken houses. In Richmond, he became a butler-chauffeur. He was thirteen when he got his driver's license. For five years, he worked for Mr. and Mrs.

Charles Gregory, of 2 River Road, driving them around the city, or answering the door as butler or waiting at table in a white coat. He describes Gregory as "a wealthy dude." Mrs. Gregory paid him two dollars and fifty cents a week, of which he unfailingly sent all but the fifty cents to his mother in South Hill. He was still in his teens when he went to work for the city.

At a program one evening at the Westwood Baptist Church, Arthur Senior met a tall, good-looking girl with long, soft hair and a face that was gentle and thin. Her name was Mattie Cunningham. People called her Baby. He soon married her. "She was just like Arthur Junior. She never argued. She was quiet, easygoing, kindhearted. She had a very strict mother, too, brother. She worked at Miller & Rhoads' department store." Asked if she sold things behind a counter, he asks back, "Are you kidding? In those days, that was impossible. . . . She read a lot. She was serious—a very serious-minded person, especially with that boy when he was first born." Arthur Junior carries his birth certificate in his wallet—July 10, 1943, "born alive at 12:55 P.M." All he remembers of his mother is an image of her standing by a door of the house in Brook Field, in a blue corduroy bathrobe, on a day when she was taken to a hospital. His father tells a story surrounding the events that followed: "In one of the oak trees outside the house, there was a bluejay bird singing up a storm. I carried Arthur Junior's mother to the hospital that morning. The bird sang for a week. I threw rocks at it. I shot at it with a .38, but not to kill it. The bird sang for a week and would not stop. A call came at five-twenty one morning from the hospital, and the bird stopped singing." His wife had been twenty-seven.

Becoming a lone parent seemed to increase in Arthur's father his already rigorous sense of discipline. When Arthur entered first grade, at the Baker Street School, near Brook Field, Mr. Ashe walked with him at the boy's pace and timed the journey. Arthur had exactly that many minutes to get home from school each day or he was in trouble. If he was late, his father took it for granted that something was wrong. In time, when Arthur wanted to work a paper route, his father would not let him do it. He thought it was too dangerous. "I kept the children home pretty close," he says. "My children never roamed the streets. A regular schedule was very important. A parent has got to hurt his own child, discipline him, hold him back from things you know aren't good for him. I don't believe in arguing and fussing. I can't stand it and never could. I don't believe in speaking two or three times, neither." He set maxims before his son like stepping stones. "You don't get nowhere by making enemies," he said. "You gain by helping others." And "Things that you need come first. Foolishness is last." "I told Arthur these things for his future, for his own good," Mr. Ashe goes on. "I told him I wanted him to get an education and get himself qualified so people could respect him as a human being. I wanted him to be a gentleman that everybody could recognize, and that's what he is right now."

It was a five-minute walk from the house in Brook Field to the house of the nearest neighbor, and to see his boyhood friends Arthur Junior would walk around the tennis courts, around the pool, through the parking yards of the Manhattan For Hire Car Company, and into the neighborhood beyond. Brook Field was encircled with light industry—the Bottled Gas Corporation of Virginia, the Valentine Meat Juice Company. "I didn't live in a so-called ghetto situation. I never saw rat-infested houses, never hung out on corners, never saw anyone knifed. I wasn't made aware of it all until I went to college. We were never poor. Not even close. Things weren't that tough for me. I've never had a job in my life. In a way, I envy people who have had. The field behind my house was like a huge back yard. I thought it was mine. Brook Field was just an athletic paradise, a dream world for a kid who likes to play sports. Tennis, baseball, horseshoes, basketball, football, swimming—you name it. The pool was so full of kids in the summer you couldn't see the water. I had no problems at all. There was really no reason in the world for me to leave the place. Everybody came to me. The athletic equipment was kept in a box in my house." Mr. Ashe spent half his time encouraging athletic games and the other half breaking up crap games. Brook Field, which has since been bulldozed and turned into the site of Richmond's new general post office, was lined and interspersed with oak trees, and Arthur, lying in bed at night during summer thunderstorms, kept waiting for lightning to shiver the big limbs, but it never did. And there was some latent fear, which surfaced now and again in remarks of Arthur Senior's, that the bottled-gas company might blow up, and that if it did the family would go with it. One night, something leaked at the gas company and two-hundred-foot flames raced into the sky. The big tanks, however, did not explode. "And that might have been the best thing that ever didn't happen to me."

Arthur's mother had taught him to read when he was four. He was an A student all through school. He never read detective stories, Westerns, or comic books. "I didn't want to waste a dime on comic books. Ridiculous. The dime would be gone in five minutes." For the most part, he read biographies and general factual writing, and he went through the World Book Encyclopedia. He read books beside the tennis courts when he wasn't playing, and he would continue this habit during tournaments in later years. In high school, he played the trumpet in a combo called the Royal Knights, but he actually mixed very little with his classmates, for his tennis increasingly took him out of their milieu. He was a good pitcher and a good second baseman, but his high-school principal, impressed by his development in tennis under Dr. Johnson, kept him from playing on the high-school baseball team. Black high schools in Richmond, in his era, had no tennis teams. Before long, and because of him, they would all have tennis teams.

Mr. Ashe's curfew during those years was 11 P.M. "Arthur, when Daddy says eleven o'clock, I mean *in* the house at eleven o'clock. See that car out that window? You're going to be driving that soon. You're going to wreck it trying to get home by eleven. You had better show me what you can do on foot before I let you drive that car." Arthur's father pondered all invitations that came Arthur's way, and screened out most of them. ("If I let him go to all the parties he was invited to, he wouldn't be where he is today.") Once, Arthur was invited to a party by a young lady whose father was a school principal and whose mother was a teacher. Arthur Senior approved of that one, and Arthur went. He was not home by eleven. His father went after him. When Mr. Ashe appeared in the doorway, the girl called out, "Hey, Art. Here is your antique father." Mr. Ashe tells this story without a smile.

Every Sunday, Arthur had to go to the Westwood Baptist Church. He refers to the experience as "a chore." "It's very tough to tell a young black kid that the Christian religion is for him," he says. "He just doesn't believe it. When you start going to church and you look up at this picture of Christ with blond hair and blue eyes, you wonder if he's on your side. When I got to college, I quit going to church. I go every once in a while now, out of curiosity." The ceramic Christ on the wall at Gum Spring has blond hair and brown eyes.

Dr. and Mrs. Graebner go to services every Sunday and to prayer meeting every Wednesday at the Cedar Hill Baptist Church, and they think that Clark is not as religious as he should be. They try to do whatever they can to bring Clark closer to God, and they always have tried to. He was a malleable child—in his mother's words, "a real nice boy, not difficult to handle, active but not mischievous." He fished for crawdads in the Rocky River, and he roller-skated around and around the blocks of Lakewood with a little neighbor named Nancy Gallo. There were no boys for

him to play with, but he didn't seem to mind. He
would always be more at ease with women than with
men. In his teens, he began to dress with what he
took to be suavity; he affected a camel's-hair coat and
looked like a mannequin from Rogers Peet. He and
his doubles partner Warren Danne chased girls together, and Warren was as impressed with Clark in
this form as he was with Clark the tennis player.
"Girls really liked him. He was *very much* at home
with them," Warren says. When Clark was sixteen
and going steady with a girl called Bubbles Keyes,
he had "total use" of the family Imperial—in effect,
his own car. When he needed money, he just asked
for it, and if the purpose was reasonable he got it.
"I was probably spoiled to some degree, as are most
only children. Now that I have mine, I can see how
easy it is to spoil a child. You love them so much."
Clark's intense concentration on tennis worried his
mother a little. She felt that he should have another
outlet, and the one she chose to encourage was figure
skating. Clark was trained at the Cleveland Skating
Club by the best available professionals, and, with his
natural sense of rhythm and his gyroscopic balance,
he became an outstanding performer. But he could
leave skating alone. He eventually had enough of
"judges dumping all over you if you were off by
one-tenth of a second—I couldn't stand that."

The Cleveland Skating Club had four cement indoor tennis courts and ten *en-tout-cas* outdoor courts, so Clark spent a high proportion of his formative years there, making the trip every afternoon on "the rapid," and going home, after office hours, with his father. (The tennis facilities are now called the Cavalry Tennis Club and are a separate, integrated organization, because "a citizen do-gooder," as Mrs. Graebner describes him, noted some years ago that the courts were on public land rented from the city, and therefore membership should be open to all. The solution was to create the Cavalry Club. Skating Club members could join Cavalry or not, as they chose, and the Graebners immediately signed up.) In his early teens, Clark became good enough to play with his father and his father's friends—"people I would consider hackers now"—and Dr. Graebner and Clark became a doubles team, competing in father-and-son tournaments. In the Western Championships, in Cleveland, they played several times against Dr. Robert Walter Johnson, of Lynchburg, and his son Robert. Clark was so young the first time that the Johnsons felt sorry for him, according to Dr. Johnson, so they eased up and gave him one game. That gave Clark the lift he needed, and the Graebners beat the Johnsons. Meeting in the same tournament in another year, the Johnsons beat the Graebners. Twice, the Graebners were national finalists in the U.S.L.T.A. father-and-son tournament. Tennis players remember how solicitous Dr. Graebner was toward Clark, and how he tried artfully to coax Clark along when he made an error. "Don't worry, honey. Don't worry, honey," Dr. Graebner would say. "Forget it. Concentrate on the next one." In later seasons, when Clark had become much the stronger player of the two, it was he who carried his father in these tournaments, and other tennis players remember that Clark used to get irked and impatient when his father missed shots, and he would grit his teeth and say to his father, "Just get me *one* point, will you?"

Clark's companion on the rest of the circuit was his mother, for Dr. Graebner had his practice and generally had to stay home. In a Chrysler New Yorker and, later, Imperials, singing along on snow tires all summer, because she felt they were safer in rain, she drove Clark and Warren Danne from Cleveland to St. Louis to Springfield to Louisville to Champaign—the cities of the tennis big-little league, where boy tennis players of the highest levels compete with one another as the season advances toward Kalamazoo. In the mind of a new American tennis player, Kalamazoo is Wimbledon. The national championships for the very young are held in August in Kalamazoo. Clark, when he was twelve, met Arthur Ashe at Kalamazoo, but, in the patterns of the draw, did not play against him. "I thought I was pretty good at twelve," Clark says. "Then I went to Kalamazoo and lost love and love in the first round. Actually, I played well. All the games went to deuce. I just didn't win them. Ray Senkowski, a six-footer who was shaving—a big Polack guy, you know—he just annihilated me, score-wise."

Clark won at Kalamazoo two years later, but meanwhile something of tangential but considerable importance would happen to him there, and to Arthur as well. Kalamazoo is often the scene of what in the career of a young tennis player is the equivalent of the day of the *alternativa* in the life of a young bullfighter—the day of his doctorate, his confirmation, his *bar mitzvah*. If a boy tennis player is good enough to show the slightest signs of world-class potential, a man inevitably approaches him at some moment at Kalamazoo and says, "Son, I'm from the Wilson Sporting Goods Company, and I'd like to give you a couple of racquets."

It could be Dunlop, Bancroft, Spalding. They're all there. It was Wilson that knighted Arthur Ashe. He was fifteen when Wilson gave him, in his words, "two racquets and a couple of covers that first time, no shoes, no strings." Since then, he has never used another kind of racquet. When he is in Chicago, he goes to the Wilson factory and picks out several dozen frames, which are put aside and sent to him, usually in lots of four, as he requests them. His Tony Trabert model used to be the Barry MacKay model, and before that the Alex Olmedo, and before that the Don Budge. It has always been the same racquet, and Ashe has used it in its various incarnations because he thinks it is the stiffest racquet that Wilson makes. "I'm a flippy player anyway. Any racquet that gives me more flip gives me trouble." He picks them out at the factory because he wants the stiffest of the stiff. He seldom breaks one, but after he has used one for a while the head gets floppy—the racquet becomes something like a riding whip—and he throws it away. He has his racquets strung at sixty pounds of tension, but no two stringing jobs are alike, so he hits with several racquets and picks out favorites. When he comes onto the court for a match, he brings two incumbent favorites, spins them, and picks one, mystically. He plays through the match with one racquet. So does Graebner. Both Ashe and Graebner say that only Pancho Gonzales and a few others change racquets frequently during a match, and they both say that Pancho is "psycho" about it. Both Ashe and Graebner use four-and-five-eighths-inch handles. Ashe is not sure what his racquet weighs. "I don't know. I don't care. Some players worry about their racquets to the quarter ounce. And they have to be strung just so. Christ, in my opinion if you worry about that crap you go out there and you can't play. You'll seldom find me with more than four racquets. I run through them, and that's it."

Graebner was anointed by Wilson, too. He was only thirteen when, at Kalamazoo, the Wilson man hit a few balls with him, then gave him two racquets and two covers. The following year, he reached the five-racquet category, and after that he went into the unlimited class. Graebner, too, has been loyal to Wilson, but Dunlop once nearly achieved him. He tried the Dunlop Maxply Fort, the racquet Rod Laver uses, and its touch impressed him. He told Wilson all about it and suggested that Wilson custom-make for him a racquet exactly like the Dunlop and paint "WILSON" on it. Wilson craftsmen built mock Dunlops for Graebner for years—until he changed to steel. This happened when Graebner, pounding away with his wooden racquet in the 1967 National Clay Court Championships, in Milwaukee, had such a bad case of tennis elbow that his elbow at the time included everything from his wrist to his shoulder. His arm felt as if it were about to fall off. He lost in singles, but he had a particular desire to hang on in the doubles, because he and his partner, Marty Riessen, had won the National Clay Court doubles twice before and could keep the trophy permanently if they won again. Graebner called Wilson in Chicago and had steel racquets rushed to Milwaukee. The steel racquet, invented by René Lacoste, was something new and unproved, but it was easy to swing, less resistant to air. It was as if a scalpel had been designed to replace a hunting knife. For Graebner, though, it was more like the sword in the stone. He and Riessen won in Milwaukee and retired the trophy; then Graebner's arm stopped hurting, and Graebner, totally committed to steel, went on to be a finalist that season at Merion, Orange, and Forest Hills—his best year ever. The tennis circuit began to glitter with steel racquets. Billie Jean King gave up wood, and to Pancho Gonzales the new racquet meant that his playing life might be extended by a couple of hundred years. The steel racquet bends like a whip when it hits, and that was just the complement Graebner needed for his firm, wrist-locked strokes. "It made me serve harder. The ball comes off the racquet so much more quickly. The stringing is different. The gut is suspended inside the frame, like a trampoline. It is a little harder to control a volley, but I shortened my backswing, because the ball climbs off the racquet so much more quickly, and now I seldom miss a return of serve. The steel racquet is the greatest thing since candy." Multitudes of hacks are now hacking with steel, but the boom that Graebner prominently helped to begin has not reached everywhere. Steel seems to have been used therapeutically where therapy was needed, but Laver still hits with his Dunlop, Ken Rosewall uses wood, and so does Arthur Ashe, who says, "Most people don't know what they're talking about when they talk about steel racquets. I'm doing fine with the wood racquet. Why should I change?"

Kalamazoo was also the probable place for initial contact between young players and the haberdashers of tennis. Ashe has been styled in free Fred Perry shirts and shorts since he was a schoolboy, and for at least as many years Graebner's *couturier* has been the versatile René Lacoste. Mrs. Graebner observed all this, and everything else at Kalamazoo, with some detachment. It occurred to her that there might be reasons that eleven- and twelve-year-olds ought not to be assembled to play for national championships. She noticed that many of the young players wept when they lost. "I thought they were a terribly intense, very emotional bunch of little boys. Arthur never showed it. He had been trained not to. But the others complained about everything. They complained about what courts they were assigned to play on. I wondered if Kalamazoo was good for them, and I still wonder. Now that I look at Clark, I think the weighing was in his favor. But if he had not got this far, I wonder if he would have been hurt." Meanwhile, she made many friends among the tennis mothers and, from sheer exposure, learned a lot about the game. She did not play it then, but she began to coach Clark with some effectiveness, because she could watch him play and tell him accurately what he was doing wrong. "You're not tossing the ball high enough. You're breaking your wrist on your forehand. On your backhand, you're swinging late."

Clark was sixteen when, at Kalamazoo, he suddenly felt such pain in his back that he could hardly hit the ball. He refused to default, and he lost, hitting a kind of crippled half stroke. His mother drove him home, and when they arrived his difficulty was so severe that he had trouble getting out of the car. He had osteochondrosis. Two of his lower vertebrae were not calcifying rapidly enough and had become, in Mrs. Graebner's words, squashed flat. Osteochondrosis characteristically attacks the upper vertebrae of prodigious young piano players, whose spinal columns bend like canes toward the keyboard. In Clark's case, the vertebrae in the small of his back were affected. Reaching high for serves had probably made the situation acute. For nearly two weeks, he had to lie flat on his back while a device was made that would surround his body like a steel birdcage from armpits to hips, held in place by a tight leather-and-canvas corset. The physician said that in the brace Clark could do anything, but when he did not wear it he would have to lie still, in bed. The day the brace came, Clark put it on and played tennis, but he could make only pathetic moves. The next day, he lost, love and love, to one of the worst players at his club. For some time after that, he played against women, and the fatigue produced by the strain of fighting the brace put circles under his eyes. Time and again he crashed to the ground, but he kept playing, and five weeks after he acquired the brace he played a match against a fairly good male opponent and—despite numerous falls—won. "That's it. I can do anything," he said to his mother. When he eventually returned to the circuit, she massaged him regularly with salve or alcohol. Other tennis players rather unsympathetically began to classify him as a "mama's boy." He wore the brace every day for fourteen months. In it, on a debilitatingly hot day—105°—in Midland, Texas, he won the National Jaycee junior-singles championship. Because he was an adolescent just coming into his full growth, the brace would influence his bearing for the rest of his life. It forced and fixed his posture. In it, he could not bend at the waist. He still doesn't. When he brushes his teeth in the morning, he places his feet apart and leans like an A-frame against the mirror. He is capable of bending at the waist, but he is out of the habit. He rarely bends to volley. He walked in the brace, as he still does, like an Etruscan warrior—his spine in absolute plumb, his chin tucked in, his implied plume flying. Graebner's walk, famous in tennis, has been almost universally interpreted as a strut.

"Look at him. He thinks he's Superman."

"Look at the way he walks."

"*Look* at the cocky bastard."

Certain aspects of Graebner's personality that occasionally surface tend to support these views, but his physical silhouette, the distinctive figure he cuts, is more relevant mechanically than psychologically. It is the signature of the osteochondrosis.

Arthur Ashe, who seems to like Graebner well enough but would not ordinarily put himself out to defend him, rises quickly when he hears unfair remarks to the effect that Graebner's success has gone to his head and then into his imperial bearing. "He appears to strut," Ashe will point out, "but he can't walk any other way."

"People have their jealousy streaks in them," Arthur's father will say. The effects upon him of his son's fame have been considerable. He says that a number of people in Richmond have become cold toward him. They never mention Arthur's success; in fact, they seem to resent it. "Some whites don't recognize Arthur Junior, and the colored are still worser. It's getting tougher and tougher all the time, in a way of speaking. I think I've lost a lot of friends. But I think I've gained some. About fifty-fifty. Some people think Arthur Junior is getting his daddy a lot of money. They say, 'That tennis player you got has really set you up, hasn't he?' " Mr. Ashe regards this as jokeworthy. His summation of the whole of Arthur's development as a tennis player is "It hung me for some money." His present landscaping and janitorial businesses grew out of odd jobs he took to help pay for Arthur's tennis. He cut grass, scrubbed floors, washed windows, and when he still didn't have enough he borrowed from the Southern Bank & Trust Co., whose branch banks he now keeps clean. Asked why he bothered to do all that, he gives an uncomplicated answer: "*Why?* Because Arthur was out there doing good." He told Arthur, "Do what you want to do, as long as you do it right. But the day you slack up is the day Daddy is going to slack up with his money."

"Arthur's Daddy promised he'd buy anything for him." (Dr. Johnson is reminiscing.) "His Daddy is a great talker, but he doesn't do everything he talks about. . . . His Daddy once had a reputation for being strictly Uncle Tom. He's moving out a bit now." Mr. Ashe says what he thinks, and he shouts when he talks about human relationships. "You respect everybody whether they respect you or not!" he bellows. "Never carry a grudge! I've seen Negroes wreck their lives through hatred of whites!" He believes out loud in law and order. "There's a certain class of people— there's a certain class of people you've got to handle by judge." For tennis tournaments in Richmond involving Arthur Junior and other high-level players, Mr. Ashe, as supervisor of tennis courts for the Department of Parks and Recreation, has set up the nets. Certain Negroes—by no means a small number—have offered him all sorts of abuse for that. They say that he is a V.I.P. and should be prominently displayed in a box seat, and should not degrade himself by working as a flunky. Driving through northside Richmond in his pickup truck past solid-looking brick houses close together on compact lots, he says that this is where the "hank-to-do," or upper-class, Negroes live, and he says that he himself is a "crooked-knees" Negro, which he defines as someone who has no class at all. "I don't have any picks and pets," he will say. "I make everybody come by me, rich or poor. If you school it out and then think back on it, you can figure that out. I respect you the same way I respect the President of the United States. If he came to my house, I'd give him the same bed you slept in. If he didn't like it, he could get the hell out.

I just want people to treat me as a human being. I'm sure my son is the same."

Ashe returns serve with a solid forehand, down the line. Graebner, lunging, picks it up with a backhand half volley. The ball floats back to Ashe. He takes a three-hundred-degree roundhouse swing and drives the ball crosscourt so fast that Graebner, who is within close reach of it, cannot react quickly enough to get his racquet on it. Hopefully, Graebner whips his head around to see where the ball lands. It lands on the line—a liner, in the language of the game. "There's Ashe getting lucky again."

Ashe does a deep knee bend to remind himself to stay low. Graebner hits a big serve wide, and a second serve that ticks the cord and skips away. Double fault. Carole pats the air. Calm down, Clark. Graebner can consider himself half broken. The score is love-thirty. Ashe thinks, "You're in trouble, Clark. Deep trouble."

"I'll bet a hundred to one I pull out of it," Graebner tells himself. Crunch. His serve is blocked back, and he punches a volley to Ashe's backhand. Ashe now has two principal alternatives: to return the ball conservatively and safely, adding to the pressure that is already heavy on Graebner, or to cut loose the one-in-ten shot, going for the overwhelming advantage of a love-forty score by the method of the fast kill. Ashe seems to have no difficulty making the choice. He blasts. He misses. Fifteen-thirty.

Graebner serves, attacks the net, volleys, rises high for an overhead—he goes up like a basketball player for a rebound—and smashes the ball away. Thirty-all.

Now the thought crosses Graebner's mind that Ashe has not missed a service return in this game. The thought unnerves him a little. He hits a big one four feet too deep, then bloops his second serve with terrible placement right into the center of the service court. He now becomes the mouse, Ashe the cat. With soft, perfectly placed shots, Ashe jerks him around the forecourt, then closes off the point with a shot to remember. It is a forehand, with top spin, sent cross-court so lightly that the ball appears to be flung rather than hit. Its angle to the net is less than ten degrees—a difficult, brilliant stroke, and Ashe hit it with such nonchalance that he appeared to be thinking of something else. Graebner feels the implications of this. Ashe is now obviously loose. Loose equals dangerous. When a player is loose, he serves and volleys at his best level. His general shotmaking ability is optimum. He will try anything. "Look at the way he hit that ball, gave it the casual play," Graebner says to himself. "Instead of trying a silly shot and missing it, he tries a silly shot and makes it." If Ashe wins the next point, he will have broken Graebner, and the match will be, in effect, even.

Again Graebner misses his first serve. Ashe, waiting for the second, says to himself, "Come on. Move in. Move in. I should get it now." When Ashe really feels he has a chance for a break, the index of his desire is that he moves in a couple of steps on second serves. He takes his usual position, about a foot behind the baseline, until Graebner lifts the ball. Then he moves quickly about a yard forward and stops, motionless, as if he were participating in a game of kick-the-can and Graebner were It. Graebner's second serve spins in, and bounces high to Ashe's backhand. Ashe strokes it with underspin. Graebner hits a deep approach shot to Ashe's backhand. Ashe hits a deft, appropriate lob. Graebner wants this point just as much as Ashe does. Scrambling backward, he reaches up and behind him and picks out of the sun an overhead that becomes an almost perfect drop shot, surprising Ashe and drawing him toward the net. At a dead run, Ashe reaches for the ball and more or less shovels it over the net. Graebner has been moving forward, too, and he has stopped for half a second, legs apart, poised, to see what will happen. The ball moves toward his backhand. He moves to the ball and drives it past Ashe, down the line. Graebner is still unbroken. But the game is at deuce. It is only the second time Ashe has extended him that far.

After this game, new balls will be coming in— all the more reason for Ashe to try to break Graebner now. Tennis balls are used for nine games (warmup counts for two), and over that span they get fluffier and fluffier. When they are new and the nap is flat, wind resistance is minimal and they come through fast and heavy. Newies, or freshies, as the tennis players call them, are a considerable advantage to the server—something like a supply of bullets. Graebner meanwhile serves wide to Ashe's forehand, and Ashe hits the return with at least equal velocity. Graebner is caught on his heels, and hits a defensive backhand down the middle. It bounces in no man's land. Ashe, taking it on his backhand, has plenty of time. His racquet is far back and ready. Graebner makes a blind rush for the net, preferring to be caught in motion than helpless on the baseline. But Ashe's shot is too hard, too fast, too tough, too accurate, skidding off the turf in the last square foot of Graebner's forehand corner. Advantage Ashe.

"Look at that shot. That's ridiculous," Graebner tells himself. He glances at Carole, who has both fists in the air. Pull yourself together, Clark. This is a big point. Graebner takes off his glasses and wipes them on his dental towel. "Stalling," Ashe mumbles.

While he is waiting, he raises his left index finger and slowly pushes his glasses into place across the bridge of his nose. "Just one point, Arthur." Graebner misses his first serve again. Ashe moves in. He hits sharply crosscourt. Graebner dives for it, catches it with a volley, then springs up, ready, at the net. Ashe lobs into the sun, thinking, "That was a good get on that volley. I didn't think he'd get that." Graebner reaches for the overhead and smashes it directly at Ashe. Ashe, swinging desperately, belts it right back at him. Graebner punches the ball away with a forehand volley. Deuce. Ashe is rattling the gates, but Graebner will not let him in. Carole has her hand on the top of her head. Unbelievable.

Graebner serves, moves up, and volleys. Ashe, running, smacks an all-or-nothing backhand that hums past Graebner and lands a few inches inside the line. Graebner says to himself, "He's hitting the lines, the lucky bastard. The odds are ten to one against him and he makes the shot. That bugs me." Advantage Ashe.

Jack Kramer, broadcasting the match, says that this is the best game not only of this match but of the entire tournament so far. Again Ashe needs just one point and he will be leading four games to two. Graebner serves. Ashe returns. Graebner half-volleys. Ashe throws a lob into the sun. Graebner nearly loses it there. He can only hit it weakly—a kind of over-head tap that drops softly at Ashe's feet. This is it. Ashe swings—a big backhand—for the kill. The ball lands two feet out. Graebner inhales about seven quarts of air, and slowly releases six. It is deuce again.

Donald Dell, the captain of the Davis Cup Team, is sitting in the Marquee. He says, "Arthur has hit five winners and he hasn't won the game. He looks perturbed." Dell knows Ashe so well that he can often tell by the way Ashe walks or stands what is going on behind the noncommittal face. But Ashe is under control. He is telling himself, "If you tend to your knitting, you will get the job done." Graebner's first serve, which has misfired seven times in this game, does not misfire now. Ashe reacts, swings, hits it hard—a hundredth of a second too late. The shot, off his backhand, fails by a few inches to come in to the sideline. Advantage Graebner.

Carole's fists are up. Clark adjusts his glasses, wipes off his right hand, and bounces the ball. He serves hard to Ashe's forehand. The ball, blasted, comes back. Disappointment races through Graeb-ner's mind. "I'm serving to his forehand. His fore-hand is his weakest shot. If the guy returns his weak-est shot all the time, he's just too good." Graebner tries a drop shot, then goes to his right on the sheer gamble that Ashe's response will take that direction. It does. Graebner, with full power, drives an apparent putaway down the line. But Ashe gets to it and blocks the ball, effecting what under the circumstances is a remarkably good lob. Graebner leaps, whips his racquet overhead, and connects. The ball hits the turf on Ashe's backhand and bounces wide. Ashe plunges for it, swings with both feet off the ground, and hits the ball so hard down the line that Graebner cannot get near it. Graebner can be pardoned if he cannot believe it. For the fourth time, the game is at deuce.

"Arthur is just seeing the ball better, or something," Graebner tells himself. But Graebner sees the ball, too, and he hits a big-crunch unplayable serve. Advantage Graebner.

Serve, return, volley—Ashe hits a forehand into the tape. Ashe has not been able to get out from under. Games are three–all, second set.

The mind of Arthur Ashe is wandering. It wanders sometimes at crucial moments. Games are six–all, second set. Ashe and Graebner have long since entered the danger zone where any major mistake can mean the loss of the set—and for Ashe, who is down one set already, the probable loss of the match. Ashe has just won three service games while losing only two points. Graebner, in his turn, has just served three games, losing no points at all. Ashe lifts the ball and hits to Graebner's forehand. Graebner answers down the line. With the premium now maximum on every shot, Ashe is nonetheless thinking of what he considers the ideal dinner—fried chicken, rice, and baked beans. During matches, the ideal dinner is sometimes uppermost in Ashe's mind. Graebner, like other tennis players, knows this and counts on it. "He'll always daydream. That's one of his big hangups. That's why he escapes to the movies so much. But in a match he won't dream long enough. I wish he would do it longer."

At these moments, Ashe thinks primarily of food, but also of parties, places he has been, things he has done, and girls, whom he dates in three colors. "This is my way of relaxing. Other people call it lack of concentration. Which is true. But I do it by habit, instinctively." Moving up with his racquet low, he picks up Graebner's forehand drive with a half volley and sends the ball, perhaps irretrievably, to Graebner's backhand corner.

There is a personally signed photograph of Richard Nixon on Graebner's desk in his apartment. Watching Nixon on television, Graebner will say, "Doesn't that make sense? How could *anyone* be more right? How could *anyone* fail to be *for* the guy?"

"Graebner is a straight, true Republican. He seems to tend that way. You think of a person, when you first meet him, in reference points. Clark is tall, strong, white, Protestant, middle-class, conservative. After a while, the adjectives fall away and he's just Clark. As far as most Negroes are concerned, whites are categorically bad until proved otherwise. My upbringing leads me to think the same way. But Clark is just Clark to me now. I don't think about it. It's just Clark over there, not a white man. I don't think he is a liberal. He's tight with his money, and he wants to see the poor work for their money. I don't entirely disagree with him, but he probably doesn't see all the ramifications. He probably doesn't care what's happening in Spanish Harlem. . . . The guy was spoiled rotten when he was a kid. All of us are spoiled to a large degree. Clark played with Charlie Pasarell, doubles. If they lost, Clark's mother said it was Charlie's fault. Clark is an only child. He's high-strung, and he can be very demanding. His speaking style sometimes sounds abrasive, staccatolike, but he doesn't mean it that way. It sounds pushy. If I'm in a bad mood, it bugs me. But I wouldn't say he's ill-tempered. There is no way you could say he is not a

nice guy if you had just met him, with no precon-
ceived notions. With his kids, he is like any father—
eager to show them off. He's a nice guy, but he has
been accustomed to instant gratification. As soon as
he wanted something, he got it. Put all this on a tennis
court, and the high-strung part, the conservative, and
the need for instant gratification become predomi-
nant."

Running flat out, Graebner hits a superb hard
backhand that surprises Ashe and slants past him to
win the point. Ashe has been thinking of food, among
other things, and did not keep his eye on the ball.
Love-fifteen. Graebner feels the surge of possibilities,
and tells himself, "I have a chance in this game. I'm
ahead now, and Arthur is sleeping."

Ashe hits a twist to Graebner's backhand, and
Graebner, instead of hitting out, chips the ball back
—the cautious thing to do.

"There is not much variety in Clark's game. It is
steady, accurate, and conservative. He makes few
errors. He plays stiff, compact, Republican tennis.
He's a damned smart player, a good thinker, but not
a limber and flexible thinker. His game is predictable,
but he has a sounder volley than I have, and a better
forehand—more touch, more power. His forehand
is a hell of a weapon. His moves are mediocre. His
backhand is underspin, which means he can't hit it

hard. He just can't hit a heavily top-spun backhand. He hasn't much flair or finesse, except in the lob. He has the best lob of any of the Americans. He's solid and consistent. He tries to let you beat yourself."

Ashe, on his way to the net, picks up the chip and hits it without exceptional force or placement to Graebner's forehand. Graebner could now probably explode one. He has what is almost a setup on his power side. But instead he tries a careful, hang-in-there, soft crosscourt top-spin dink, and it is Ashe who explodes. The orthodox way to hit a volley is to punch it, with a backswing so short that it begins in front of the player's body. Ashe now—characteristically—draws his racquet back as far as he can reach and volleys the ball with a full, driving swing. The impact is perfect, and the ball goes past Graebner's feet like a bullet fired to make him dance. "I hit too soft and short," Graebner tells himself. "That's the difference between playing on one level and playing on another. You've got to hit it *authoritatively*." Fifteen–all.

Ashe hits a big serve. He is not day-dreaming now. Graebner blocks back a good return. Ashe, moving in, must half-volley. The shot should be deep—to protect his position, his approach to the net. Instead, he tries one of the most difficult shots in tennis. Basically, it is a foolhardy shot. It is not a percentage shot, and is easier to miss than to make. Players call it a half-volley drop shot. Ashe reaches down, lightly touches the rising ball, and sends it on a slow, sharply angled flight toward the net. The risk is triple—hitting the net, missing the placement, and leaving a sitter for Graebner to put away if he should be able to get to the ball. The ball settles down to a landing in Graebner's forecourt. Graebner is headed for it at top speed, and he almost gets there in time. He drives the ball into the umpire's chair, and straightens up with a disgusted look on his face. Ashe's half-volley drop shot was the sort of thing a person should try once a match, if at all, and hardly in the most vital moments of the second set, when—already losing—he is in imminent peril of falling almost hopelessly behind. It was a loose flick shot, requiring tremendous ball control, and Ashe, in Graebner's view, was very lucky to succeed with it. "How can he do it?" Graebner asks himself. His shoulders droop as he walks back to the baseline. Thirty-fifteen.

"I've never been a flashy stylist, like Arthur. I'm a fundamentalist. Arthur is a bachelor. I am married and conservative. I'm interested in business, in the market, in children's clothes. It affects the way you play the game. He's not a steady player. He's a wristy slapper. Sometimes he doesn't even know where the ball is going. He's carefree, lacksadaisical, forgetful.

His mind wanders. I've never seen Arthur really discipline himself. He plays the game with the lacksadaisical, haphazard mannerisms of a liberal. He's an underprivileged type who worked his way up. His family are fine people. He's an average Negro from Richmond, Virginia. There's something about him that is swashbuckling, loose. He plays the way he thinks. My style is playmaking—consistent, percentage tennis—and his style is shotmaking. He won't grub around. He doesn't gut out a lot of points where he has to work real hard, probably because he is concerned about his image. He doesn't want to appear to be a grubber. He comes out on the court and he's tight for a while, then he hits a few good shots and he feels the power to surge ahead. He gets looser and more liberal with the shots he tries, and pretty soon he is hitting shots everywhere. He does not play percentage tennis. Nobody in his right mind, really, would try those little dink shots he tries as often as he does. When he hits out, he just slaps. He plays to shoot his wad. He hits the ball so hard that it's an outright winner or he misses the shot. When he misses, he just shrugs his shoulders. If he were more consistent, he might be easier to play. Negroes are getting more confidence. They are asking for more and more, and they are getting more and more. They are looser. They're liberal. In a way, 'liberal' is a synonym for 'loose.' And that's exactly the way Arthur plays. I've always kidded him, saying, 'If the Negroes take over, please make me a lieutenant. Not a general or a colonel. Just a lieutenant.' "

Lieutenant Ashe, USA, professes to enjoy the irony of this request, and promises to do what he can. He endorses Graebner's analysis of his game, and says, "To put it simply, I just blast the ball back and the point's over. Of course, I miss a lot. Tennis is a means to an end, that's all. If I could really be what I wanted to be, I would love to be a pro quarterback." He lifts the ball and hits another hard first serve at Graebner. Almost an ace, it jerks Graebner far off balance, but he hits it back solidly, up the middle. Ashe, moving up, is again confronted with the need to half-volley. For the second time in a row, instead of hitting the deep, correct ball, he tries to pull a drop shot off the grass, and for the second time in a row he succeeds. "*Another* half-volley drop shot!" Donald Dell comments. "How loose can you get?" Graebner, sprinting, gets to this one, barely, and more or less pushes it down the line—a remarkable effort—but Ashe, standing straight up and not even bothering to stroke with form, flips a slow, looping crosscourt wood-shot forehand into Graebner's court and just beyond his reach—a stroke that might have been made with a broom handle. Forty-fifteen.

Graebner slams his racquet down onto the turf. He shouts, "God damn it, Arthur, you're so lucky!" To anyone who can halfway read lips, the sentiment goes out over national TV. Ashe stands quietly. He does not show the pleasure he must feel. He bounces the ball six times with his racquet, and he shoves his glasses back up his nose. "Graebner is now completely infuriated," Dell continues. "Look at him—the Greek tragic hero always getting pushed around by the gods. He really sees himself that way, and it's his greatest weakness." Graebner has been known to do a great deal more than slam his racquet down, spit sour grapes, and take the Prime Mover's name in vain. He has been a behavioral case study in a game in which—at least among Americans—brattishness seems to be generic. Apparently, he feels that he can accurately assign blame outside himself for almost every shot he misses, every point he loses. He glowers at his wife. He mutters at other people in the crowd. Airplanes drive him crazy. Bad bounces are personal affronts. He glares at linesmen. He carps at linesmen. He intimidates ball boys. He throws his racquet from time to time, and now and then he takes hold of the fence around a court and shakes it violently, his lips curling. He seems to be caged. The display of misery that he can put on is too convincing not to be genuine. If his opponent makes a great shot, Graebner is likely to mutter a bitter aside, then turn and say "Good shot" with mechanical magnanimity. He has shouted four-letter obscenities at people in the grandstands, and in the Australian National Championships one year he told an umpire to shut up. At Longwood in 1966, he swatted a ball at a linesman about twenty feet away from him. The ball didn't harm the man, perhaps because it didn't hit him.

Ashe is detached about Graebner in a way that some tennis players are not when they talk about him. "When things go wrong, Clark can't seem to resist saying or doing something that shows dissatisfaction, to put it mildly," Ashe says. "I think it has sunk in that he sometimes offends people, and I can see him fighting it, trying to correct it." Tennis players frequently compare Graebner to Dr. Jekyll and Mr. Hyde, the essence of what they say being that he is a completely different, friendly, smiling person away from a tennis court, and that off the court of late he has obviously made a particular effort to be nice. Graebner's friend Warren Danne has always enjoyed his company off the court, but says that "Clark has behaved like an ass on the court since he was eighteen." Dr. Graebner argues that Clark is merely ignoring an irrational ethic. "Just because someone once wrote that this is a gentleman's game, you have no right to blow up like any full-blooded desirous person," Dr. Graebner says. "Tennis is a business. Tennis isn't fun. The opportunities tennis gives are tremendous, but not at no cost to the individual."

"He has gone out of his way to be a good boy," his mother says. "Basically, I don't know of any better boy all around than Clark has been. He was never a problem, never a bad teen-ager.

"He has always tried to be what we have wanted him to be, what he felt he should be, what he felt we would have liked him to be," his father says. "He makes friends wherever he goes. He has more friends than you can shake a stick at."

"Someone should have sat on him when he was young," Clark's wife says. "Officials threatened him but did not act. No one blocked him."

"He's very German," Warren Danne goes on. "I don't think I've met anyone in this country who's more German than Graebner—clean, positive, always moving forward. I don't think he debates alternatives. He sees things one way and acts."

There is perhaps something Germanic about Herr Graebner on a tennis court. His kills are clean, but when he kills he tends to overkill. His overhead is hit with his whole arm—no mere flick of the wrist. The arm comes down like the moving part of a paper cutter. "One fell swoop of the arm and the ball is gone," Ashe says. "And I think he enjoys hitting his forehands as hard as he can. He can hit them harder than anyone else playing, I think." Graebner likes to hit drop shots, and when other players race to them and make desperate gets he stands at the net and crunches their feeble returns—a standard thing to do, except that other players sometimes believe that the direction the ball takes indicates that Graebner is trying to kill them. They have stopped in the middle of matches to ask Graebner what he thinks he is doing. "Graebner will sometimes literally hit the ball through you," Ashe will say. "If you don't get out of the way, he'll hurt you with it."

Graebner has won cups for sportsmanship. At crucial moments in crucial matches, he has stepped to the umpire's chair to say that a point apparently his should be credited to his opponent, because his racquet ticked the ball. After hitting the ball at the linesman in 1966, he was suspended from the United States Davis Cup Team. The team—Ashe was on it— went to Pôrto Alegre without Graebner, and the United States lost miserably to Brazil. "Clark felt that this was a way that God was looking out for him," his wife reveals. "Instead of being away when we had our first baby, he was at home and he was not in on the disgrace of losing in Brazil. He has always been very religious." The day he was suspended happened to be Clark Graebner Day in Beachwood, Ohio, his home town.

"Arthur's manners have always been quiet and restrained on the tennis court," Graebner says. "What I wonder is: Would he have been that way if he had been white? For me, there was always the spoiled-brat thing. I probably *was* a brat, to some extent. People have called me—and a lot of others—spoiled brats. Would it have been the same for Arthur? He has had to master the restraint of his emotions on the court. In fact, I think he works too hard at trying to keep his cool. He comes off the court after winning a title and gives it the cool play. It's not human to be that cool. He is penned in. Feelings need an outlet. I hope he is not going to lose his cool by trying to keep his cool."

For many years, within the strict dimensions of Dr. Johnson's approach to white tennis, Ashe played under the disadvantage of stifling his reactions, of never complaining, of calling close ones against himself. Now the training is paying off. When things get tough, he has control. His latent confidence—his cool—works in his favor. Even in very tight moments, other players think he is toying with them. They rarely know what he is thinking. They can't tell if he's angry. It is maddening, sometimes, to play against him.

He has said that what he likes best about himself on a tennis court is his demeanor. "I strive to cultivate it. It's a conversation point. It's a selling point. 'He's icy and he's elegant. Imperturbable.' What it is is controlled cool, in a way. Always have the situation under control, even if losing. Never betray an inward sense of defeat." He once lost in the finals of the Australian National Championship when a foot fault was called against him on the last point of the match. Almost any other American player would have instantly turned into flaming gasoline. Ashe came very close to it, but he kept control. "You must expect four or five bad calls a match," he says. "A match can be won or lost on a bad call." About as close as he will come to complaining is to stare evenly for a moment at a linesman. In an extreme case, he may walk to the point just outside the line where he believes his opponent's shot landed and draw a little circle around the spot with the handle of his racquet.

"I used to have a hang-loose attitude," he will say. "That suggests a don't-care attitude. If I won, fine; if I didn't win, too bad. But you just *have* to care—about anything you have to do. You appreciate excellence for excellence's sake." It is part of his cool that he almost never lets himself say or show how much he loves the game he plays, but one has only to watch him on the courts at West Point, playing with the cadet varsity tennis players, to see the extent of his athletic generosity and his affection for what he is doing. He gives away points when he knows that the cadets will not suspect him. He plays at a minor pace with a spectacular suggestion of high effort. He mixes encouragement with instruction and humor in an unending stream of words across the net. "When you run for a ball that's real wide, you run as if you were going to take one more step when you get there. One more step and you would have had it," he will say. Or, "One of the best shots against a man at the net is to hit it right at him. If he's standing there and you hit it hard right at him, what the hell is he going to do?"

As a cadet's good shot goes past him, he shouts, "That's just too tough!" But, of course, he is realistic with the cadets. He doesn't want to hurt them, or waste his own effort. So he always wins. "I am really happy in this game sometimes," he will admit. "One time I am really happy is when the last point is over in a tournament and I have won. Five minutes later, however, it's all gone."

He lifts the ball and hits a deep, flat serve at Graebner down the middle—too deep. Fault. He goes up to serve again, deciding, "I might try to fool him by hitting to the other side, even if I waste a point." He hits a slice so hard and with such sharp placement, close to the sideline, that the ball jumps cleanly past Graebner's racquet for a service ace. "Way to go, Art, baby," Ashe says to himself, and he walks to the umpire's chair and reaches for a cool, damp towel. Game to Lieutenant Ashe. He leads, seven games to six, second set.

"I don't know how deeply rooted Arthur's feelings are. I would guess they are getting deeper at the moment. He's going to be very wrapped up in civil rights. He's got to come through that first. The question is: Is he going to make a business out of civil rights, or is he going to be a businessman and give time to civil rights? Is he going to be a devotee of a belief, or is he going to attend to a business career? He works now, part time, for Philip Morris Interna-national—a job he got as a result of tennis. I got my job with Hobson Miller through tennis, but even without tennis I would have had a good job, through my background and social contacts. With his poor, liberal Democratic background, he has to be always striving to get ahead, striving for recognition, and he is achieving something daily through his tennis conquests. I think he'll stay with Philip Morris. I think he's too selfish not to want to *be* somebody at the age of thirty-five. Of course, he's never going to be chairman of the board, or president. He'll be a brand manager, or a vice-president in charge of marketing, making fifty or sixty thousand a year. That's an easy way to go. It's a lot easier to make half a fortune than a whole fortune. Even though Arthur is well accepted in a place like Philip Morris, he's never going beyond that level. I accept Arthur any way, but many people don't. He's accepted only because he's a tennis player. If the West Side Tennis Club rejected Dr. Bunche, they're going to reject him. Meanwhile, he'll get married around age twenty-eight and have three kids. I think he's too smart to marry a white girl. That's a headache. If he marries a white girl, who's going to house him? He'll live in a very lovely residence somewhere, but I don't know where. I don't know where a Negro executive lives in New York. I don't even know. I don't know where they live. I just don't know."

"I think I might live in Europe for a while. In Spain or Sweden. I go out now and then with a Swedish tennis player. Her name is Ingrid. She really enjoys life. It's unbelievable. If two people are in love, they're cowards not to get married. In general, though, I lean toward a Negro girl. It's easier. I haven't the slightest idea what I am going to be doing twenty years from now. Graebner will still be in New York. His daughter and his son will have gone to the best private schools. His son will be at Princeton or Yale. Clark will be a member of the Knickerbocker

Club, or one of those. He'll just be living the quiet, middle-class life. He'll be the president of that paper company if he tends to his knitting. I'll probably be something like Jackie Robinson, involved in business and politics. I'd like to be in business for myself. I have my hopes—for financial security, for three or four children. What else is there to life besides a family and financial security?"

"If I could, right now, I would join the Racquet Club or the River Club, but these things take time and can't be hurried. I don't want to be just a fifty-to-sixty-thousand-a-year man. I don't know if I'm shrewd, but if I see an opportunity I'll try to take advantage of it. If I had to bet on it, I would say I have a good opportunity to be a millionaire by forty, or perhaps even somewhere on the thirty-five-to-forty plateau. I'll be living in Manhattan, Greenwich, or Scarsdale then. My kids will have gone to Chapin, Spence, Trinity—the best schools—and on to Lawrenceville, Williams, Vassar, Northwestern. Carole will be active in the Junior League—that type of circle. I'll be the president of Hobson Miller and on the board of Saxon Industries, the mother company. I'll play tennis a little, and, hopefully, belong to the Racquet Club and the River Club. Hopefully, I will have made a lot of money and have no qualms about the way I've done it. One thing I'll always try to do is keep religion in the forefront of the children's minds. That I regard as very, very important. If you lead the type of life that the Lord wants you to lead, He'll give to you. Things come to those who profess and believe."

Graebner, standing with Ashe by the umpire's chair while exchanging ends, rubs sawdust on his racquet handle to dry it and keep it from slipping in his grip. "Thank God I never have trouble with my handle," Ashe remarks, and returns to the court. Graebner eventually follows, and serves. The ball is too fast to be playable. Ashe gets his racquet on it but deflects it low, into the net. Fifteen-love.

Graebner serves wide. Ashe stretches to hit a cross-court backhand. Graebner volleys from his own backhand—a deep, heavy ball. Ashe flips a lob into the air. Both players now make tactical errors. Graebner decides that the ball is on its way out, and fails to pick the overhead out of the air. The ball drops safely within the baseline, and Graebner desperately sprints around it and drives it with his backhand. Ashe, meanwhile, has watched all this in fascination and has forgotten to go to the net to position himself to destroy what has to be a vulnerable return. As it happens, though, Graebner's shot lands several inches out of bounds. "I'm one of the luckiest guys around," Ashe tells himself. Fifteen-all.

Graebner rocks and hits, and Ashe lets the serve go by. He thinks it ticked the cord and is a let. He waits for official confirmation of this, but none comes. The serve is an official ace. Thirty-fifteen.

Ashe says nothing, and walks to the other side of the court to await Graebner's next one. He sends it back down the line. Graebner, coming to the ball about a foot behind the service line, volleys it on his forehand—into the net. "Can you imagine *me* hitting a shot like that?" Graebner asks himself. "Lazy. Lazy. Bad volley. I was too far back. I should have been in another two feet." The set itself is now hanging on one or two threads. Graebner has the commanding advantage of the serve. Ashe has the unnerving advantage of being within two points of winning. The pressure is total in both directions. Carole's fists are up. Come on, now. This is a big point. Thirty–all.

Graebner rocks. Hits. Fault. He serves again, safely, in the middle of the box, and Ashe, who has not moved in on the serve, hits a backhand up the middle—so far so conservative on both sides of the net. Graebner half-volleys to Ashe, on the baseline, in the middle. Ashe loosens. He drives the ball to Graebner's forehand. Graebner punches back hard a volley down the line. Ashe is on it with speed, his racquet back. He hits a flippy backhand, acutely angled crosscourt, with lots of top spin and lots of risk. There is no possibility of Graebner's getting near it but every possibility that the shot will go out. It's a liner. It leaves chalk dust in the air. Ashe turns, in the cascade of applause for his sensationally incautious shot, and walks away from the court. He withdraws into himself, his back to the court and to Graebner. Thirty-forty. Set point.

"Look at him going away from the court, away from the situation," says Donald Dell. "Believe me, he never does that. He's nervous. Think of the pressure on him. And still he hits a shot like that one. That's why he's a great tennis player. It's like a pro quarterback when he is down six points, third and twenty on his own forty, forty-two seconds to go, and he throws a pass into the end zone. The big play at the right time. He not only tries it, he makes it."

Graebner hits his big serve to Ashe's forehand, and Ashe drives the ball into the umpire's chair. But the serve was a couple of inches out. Graebner serves again, and Ashe's low, underspun return drops in the service box. Graebner moves up and hits to Ashe's backhand. Ashe gets set to hit. He can do anything out of his backhand backswing, and now he seems to be preparing for a dink or a drop shot. But he is faking, to draw Graebner in. Graebner runs for the net. Ashe lobs. Graebner is moving one way and the ball, above him, is moving the other way. It drops fifteen inches inside the line. The set is over. The match is even.

"He fooled me completely. I had no idea," Graebner says to himself.

Ashe is saying to himself, "I think I'm going to win it all."

"A set apiece. I'm still in there," Graebner thinks. He looks worried.

Ashe bounces the ball ten times, while applause subsides, and then he pushes his glasses into place, lifts the ball, and hits an uncomplicated ace that splits the court. He hits another ace. And with four additional shots he wins the first game of the third set.

When Ashe's alarm clock sounds, he gets out of bed, goes sleepily to his bureau, picks up his can of Burma Blockade, squirts himself twice under the arms, and says, "What's happening?" This occurs every morning. Sometimes he stumbles as he crosses the room, because any number of objects may be on the floor. There is always an open, half-filled suitcase somewhere. Tennis clothes fan out of it like laundry spread to dry. Racquets are all over the place, strung and unstrung—on the floor, on bookshelves, under the bed. "I hate orderliness," he will say. There are piles of unanswered letters. His conscience tells him to answer them all. Ripped envelopes are so numerous that they should probably be removed with a rake. There is a stack of copies of the Richmond *Afro-American*. Tennis trophies are here and there like unwashed dishes—West of England Lawn Tennis Championships; U.S. National Clay Court Men's Singles Winner 1967. His books are more or less concentrated on bookshelves, but some can also be found on or under every other piece of furniture in the room. They have accumulated during the time—fourteen months—he has been living in the Bachelor Officers' Quarters at the United States Military Academy. Under his bed is "Report of the National Advisory Commission on Civil Disorders." On a chair near his pillow are "Fundamentals of Marketing" and "The Autobiography of Malcolm X." Along the shelves go "Human Sexual Response," "Black Power," "Emily Post's Etiquette," "Contract Bridge for Beginners," "Ulysses," "The Rise and Fall of the Third Reich," "The Confessions of Nat Turner," "The Human Factor in Changing Africa," "Paper Lion," "Mata Hari," "Dynamic Speed Reading," "The Naked Ape," "The New York Times Guide to Personal Finance," "Marketing Management, Analysis and Planning," "A Short History of Religions," "Elementary French," "Spanish in Three Months,"

"Aussie English," and "U.S. Equal Employment Opportunity Commission Hearings—N.Y., N.Y. 1968." A roommate once cleaned the place up—picked up the clothes, stacked all the racquets, and arranged the books—and Ashe said, "This room is so neat I can't stand it."

The Graebners' apartment, on East Eighty-sixth Street, is trim and orderly, with comfortable new, non-period furniture and a TV set that rolls on wheels. The apartment is a module many floors up in a modern concrete hive. The hall outside is narrow, and all the doors along it are made of hollow steel and have peepholes. Graebner has been reading "The Arrangement" ("just for trash"), "The Effective Executive" (because that is exactly what he would like to be), a biography of Richard Nixon, "The Rich and the Super-Rich," "Airport" ("for more trash"), and "The Pro Quarterback." Graebner is less verbal than Ashe. Graebner's language is casual and idiomatic. A word like "phraseology" will come out of him in four syllables, and if Ashe happens to hear it he is likely to call Graebner's attention to the error, for Ashe is meticulous about some things, and language is one. Ashe is very literal. In restaurants, for example, the Davis Cup Team trainer is forever asking waitresses for "diet sugar," and Ashe will say, "Diet *sugar*? Diet sweetener, maybe." He says he would like to write. Meanwhile, he does the *Times* crossword puzzle every day and drives himself crazy until he has it complete and correct. He calls up friends long distance to ask for help if he needs it. When they ask him why he does the crossword with such energy, he will say something like "I'm not sure. It may give me a false sense of intellectual security."

The door of Ashe's clothes closet is always open, and the light in there has been on for fourteen months. Love beads hang on a hook on the door. Ashe looks extremely contemporary when he goes off to New York for a date wearing the beads, a yellow turtleneck, and what he calls his "ru" jacket. More often, he just looks trim and conventional, like Graebner, in a business suit. In uniform, he is the model soldier —salutes and does all the things an officer is supposed to do. He seems to get pleasure out of it. It would probably be an exaggeration to say that he enjoys the West Point life, but he plays the game. He works hard when he is on the post. He gets up at seven and is at his desk by eight. Graebner works even harder. A million dollars must seem a long way off when you can't even get an American Express credit card. Graebner applied and was turned down, apparently on the ground of insufficient visible income—to the limitless amusement of all the other players on the Davis Cup Team. Ashe and Graebner are both extraordinarily conscious of the stock market, and each thinks he is a shrewd investor. An amateur tennis player at their level can have something to invest, since he can collect in expenses and sundry compensations as much as twenty thousand dollars a year. Ashe never misses the *Times'* stock-market quotations, and as his eye runs through them he says, "Too tough. . . . Fantastic. . . . Unbelievable." Graebner has three brokers. He describes them as "a conservative, a middle-of-the-roader, and a flier." The conservative is his mother's broker, in Cleveland. The middle-of-the-roader is a man in Richmond whom Graebner met on the tennis circuit. The flier was a friend of Graebner's at Northwestern and now works in New York for Smith, Barney & Co. When tennis takes Graebner to a place like Las Vegas or San Juan, he goes to the gaming tables and hangs on every roll of the dice as if he were in the semifinals of the United States Open Championships. Ashe is a few feet up the velvet, behaving the same way.

New balls come into the match. Graebner hits three unmanageable serves. He quickly raises the score to one–all, third set.

As amateurs, Ashe and Graebner qualify for none of the prize money that is available to professionals in this tournament. Noting this, an anonymous woman feels such pity for Ashe that she sends him a hundred shares of General Motors common. One evening, Graebner learns about it from Ashe.

"A *hundred* shares of General *Mo*tors!" Graebner says, and his vocal cords seem tight.

"That's right," Ashe tells him. "From an anonymous donor."

"White or Negro?"

"I don't know. She saw me play and felt sorry for me."

"How much is it a share—forty dollars?"

"Hell, no. Ninety-five."

"She gave you *nine thousand five hundred dollars?*"

"You better believe it."

"That's too tough. Why didn't she give it to me? I deserve it as much as you. You son of a bitch, you owe me four thousand seven hundred and fifty dollars."

Graebner appears to be somewhat tense under the pressure of not being able to do much against Ashe's serve, which is becoming perceptibly stronger. In the last ten games that Ashe has served, Graebner has won only nine scattered points. Ashe double-faults. Graebner looks happy. Ashe takes four straight points, including one on a loose, liberal, infuriating touch shot. Graebner mutters, "Arthur, you lucky bastard. How can you hit that shot?" Game to Lieutenant Ashe. He leads, two games to one.

Donald Dell once asked Graebner to name his best friends in tennis. "I don't have any friends in tennis," Graebner answered. Dell says that Graebner becomes suspicious when someone likes him. "I don't have too many friends, period," Graebner has also said. "I like to escape, to go on my own. I'm not one of those kind of guys that needs people around him all the time. I hate to put on a façade. I don't enjoy it. It's too tough. I feel pretty close to guys like Arthur and Charlie Pasarell, because of the camaraderie we've had in growing up together. Mr. Miller, my boss, has become a very, very, very close friend, kind of a fatherly friend, but I don't confide in anyone my own age."

Charlie Pasarell could be almost anyone's best friend. He is a Puerto Rican, tall, handsome, thoughtful, agreeable, generous, sleepy, and hedonistic, who grew up near San Juan. Banana trees grow beside his swimming pool, which has tiled racing lanes. His family is rich, and prominent in Puerto Rico. Charlie developed as a tennis player on the courts of the Caribe Hilton. On the junior circuit in the United States, he sometimes travelled in the Graebners' car, and now and then he stayed in their home. He has known Graebner and Ashe as long as they have known each other. The three are about the same age, play the same game technically, and are a vintage of American tennis. Ashe is national amateur champion. Graebner is (and Ashe has been) national clay-court champion. Pasarell has twice been national indoor champion. Pasarell is the only tennis player in the history of Wimbledon to have beaten a Wimbledon defending champion on Wimbledon's opening day. He and Ashe have at different times been ranked No. 1 in the United States, and Graebner has been ranked No. 2. Now a private in the Army, stationed at Stewart Air Force Base, in Newburgh, New York, Pasarell has a room there that consists of several square yards of linoleum, some steel lockers, and a cot. So he spends a great deal of time in Ashe's suite at West Point, enjoying the perquisites of an officer's life with none of the responsibilities. Ashe and Pasarell were college roommates—the No. 2 and No. 1 tennis players, respectively, for U.C.L.A.—and ever since those years they have been inseparable. On a tennis court, Pasarell can drive Graebner out of his mind, because he sometimes waits until Graebner has him at or near match point before he opens up his full game and fights back to win—as he did in the finals of the most recent Eastern Grass Court Championships, at Orange. Pasarell has been behind Graebner two sets, five games to none, and forty-love, with Graebner serving, only to turn around and beat him, and cause Graebner to shake the fences in outrage. "As long as I live, I will never understand the Latin temperament," Graebner once said at such a moment.

"I would love to play you in the finals of any tournament" was Pasarell's amiable response. "The more pressure there is, the better my chances would be."

Graebner once asked Pasarell how he could conceivably style himself a Democrat. "You're from the social class, the inbred class, and you're wealthy," Graebner said. "Don't you want to protect what you have? I can see a man like Jimmy Ling, of Ling-Temco-Vought, being a Democrat, because he wants contracts with the government. But I can't see why anyone else—you, H. L. Hunt, my father—should want to contribute to things like Medicare and Medicaid. How can you be a Democrat?"

"Conscience is more important than money," Pasarell said.

Pasarell once observed, "Tennis is a fight of character. A couple of good shots can build the spirit. It used to be impossible to get into a match with Arthur, because there was no character in his game. It was like hitting against a backboard. He was just out there hitting balls. He either hit or missed. If he was missing, he lost. If he was hitting, he won. It seemed to suit him either way. You have to put some heart into many things. Arthur sometimes hasn't. We once took a three-hour exam in a course at U.C.L.A. and Arthur walked out after forty-five minutes. I told him later that I had found the exam extremely difficult, and he said, 'You must be kidding.' He got a B. He would have done better if he had got involved. He majored in marketing, but his favorite course was anthropology. He thinks out loud, and, without meaning to, he used to hurt people's feelings. He was indiscreet, saying things that embarrassed his friends. The usual view of him is that he is cool, even-tempered, and unemotional, and this is right to a certain extent. His dad taught him to be humble, quiet, to live and let live, and that others are entitled to their opinions. His father was protective of Arthur—because of racial prejudice and because Arthur's mother died when he was so young—and Arthur developed a shield. He would never let anything grab him emotionally. He would accept things as they occurred. I consider him my best friend and I think I am his best friend, but if I had gone to him and said, 'I have a bullet in my stomach,' he would have said, 'What else is new?' He would have cared, but he wouldn't have shown it. His character *and* his tennis are different now. He still has the ability to go for the outright shot from any position at any time, and this is why some players are petrified of him. But he plays more percentage tennis, too. He will dink. He spins his first serve in more, instead of going for the outright ace. He'll block his return of serve, instead of always hitting away. He'll fake a little bit. He'll intimidate. He'll slice. He'll lob. He'll take speed off his passing shots. His volleys are more consistent. He's alive now. He is more concerned about things— about racial problems, family, business, his friends, his game. He is a little more careful now of what he does. He's more involved in the match, more emotionally involved, and that is why he has become a great, great tennis player."

Games are two–all, third set. Ashe, hurrying again, double-faults for the fifth time. Nonetheless, there is nothing stiff about the way he walks. He remains loose and limber. Love-fifteen.

In an automobile, Ashe does not like to be a passenger, and he will go to any lengths to avoid making a trip in which he is not the driver. He explains that it is his belief that even in a context of reasonable speeds he can move an automobile from one place to another faster than the next man. He owns a red Mustang, and wants to put a telephone in it. He is bored easily, hates routine work, and hates wasting time. He wants to complete anything he starts absolutely without delay. Now he bounces the ball twice, snaps his wrist at the high pivot of his swing, and hits a serve down the middle that is too much for Graebner. Fifteen-all.

Graebner has hypochondriacal tendencies, and other tennis players call him Hypo. He worries about drafts, coughs, hiccups, sore throats, and colds, and mistakes muscle twinges for coronary thromboses. He sticks a finger *inside* the necks of freshly opened Coca-Cola bottles and rubs them "clean" before he drinks. Before almost any match, he makes remarks about the several besetting ailments that happen to be uppermost in his mind at the time.

It is doubtful whether a trimmer, healthier, better-built, or more powerful human being than Graebner has ever stood on a tennis court. Ashe serves to his forehand—a dangerous thing to do—and Graebner muscles one down the line so fast that Ashe's volley makes a high, awkward parabola and lands beyond the baseline. Graebner has Ashe down fifteen-thirty, and is thinking, "I have a great chance for a break here."

Ashe's signature—"Arthur R. Ashe, Jr."—is about halfway between bold and timid, and well within the sub-Hancock zone. Graebner's signature, full of sweep and dash, is pi Hancock squared. The "G" is two and a quarter inches high. He waits, a foot behind the baseline, for Ashe's serve. It is wide. And now Graebner knows that Ashe's second serve will almost certainly be a twist to the backhand. If Graebner wins this point, he will damage Ashe's morale and set himself up to break through in the game. Ashe will be down fifteen-forty, and Graebner will have the match in his control. Ashe lifts the ball, hits, and the twist falls exactly where Graebner had imagined it would. He decides to detonate—to go, as Arthur surely would, for the big point with a single bold shot. He swings and hits it—a flat backhand. At twice the speed necessary to win, the ball goes down the line, but on the out side. Thirty-all.

Graebner seldom goes to the movies. Ashe seems to spend more time in movie theatres than he does on tennis courts. From all the films he has seen, the two characters who seem to remain most prominently in his mind are "the guy in 'A Thousand Clowns,' because he is self-taught and doesn't give a damn about society," and Zorba the Greek, "because *he* doesn't give a damn about society, either, but would go out of his way to help you." Certain symbols mean a great deal to Graebner. He can identify a pair of Gucci shoes a block away. Tennis travelling takes him to as many as five continents a year, but he says he is not interested in sightseeing anywhere. Ashe is an aggressive tourist, with a movie camera over his arm, sunglasses over his eyes, and an article on Afghanistan—or wherever—in his hand. He says that Charlotte Amalie reminds him of Tasmania. Australia is "unbelievable," a sporting fantasia, by his report, because the only news of Australia that he has ever seen on the front pages of Australian newspapers is news of sports. "Australian English is a barroom language," he will say. "It is not a language for a woman."

Ashe and Graebner would rather win the Davis Cup together than win Forest Hills as individuals. "Tournaments are no sweat, but you lose sleep in the Davis Cup," Ashe says. "If you lose a tournament, it's just *you* losing. If you lose in the Davis Cup, the United States has lost."

"It's patriotism," Graebner says. "I'd rather win in the Davis Cup than win Wimbledon." He gets goose pimples when he hears "The Star-Spangled Banner." Sometimes the Davis Cup Team's daily training exercises are declared optional, and when that happens Graebner is likely to be the only one who does them.

When Graebner is off the court, his mind sometimes wanders in the way that Ashe's does in action. Graebner frequently clicks off in the middle of conversations, but he is not thinking about ideal dinners. Ashe, if he is in New York, trains on soul food at places with names like the West Boondock Lounge.

Once in a while, he will have a glass of beer with a shot of lime juice in it. Graebner, during Forest Hills, eats big breakfasts, has soup and tea for lunch, and eats the same training meal every night—a vodka Martini, a shrimp cocktail, a baked potato without salt or butter, and roast beef or steak. Neither Ashe nor Graebner smokes. It has been many years since Budge Patty, deciding to take his tennis seriously, bought a pair of scissors so that he could cut his cigarettes in half.

Ashe slices his first serve in, follows it, and volleys deep and hard to Graebner's backhand corner. Graebner reaches on the run and makes an underhanded save, flicking the ball into the air in a short and immensely vulnerable lob. Ashe, standing at the crossroads in the middle of the service line, points in the overhead and drives it down Graebner's throat. Scrambling far behind the baseline, Graebner makes an unbelievable retrieve and sends up another lob— this one very high and deep. It comes down with wind drift and lands by the sideline, one inch out. Graebner shows his disappointment but does not look at Carole. His great chance appears to have left him. Forty-thirty.

Ashe pushes up his glasses, wipes his chin on his shoulder, bounces the ball twice, and hits his flat maximum serve precisely into the corner where the service line and the sideline meet. The closest the ball comes to Graebner is fifteen feet. Graebner never moves or lifts his racquet. Ace. Game to Ashe. He leads, three games to two.

Coming into a room—any room, anywhere—the first thing Ashe says is "What's happening?" When he ends a conversation, he says, "Well, it's been nice talking to you." These are the frames of his relationships with other people—these expressions, and a habit he has of wearing sunglasses indoors. They keep the world at one remove. The sunglasses are uneroded bits of the shield that Pasarell talks about. "I don't mind being by myself," Ashe will say. "I prefer the company of people I'm interested in, but I don't seek out people just to be with people. Jesus, sometimes it's exactly the opposite. Music is my best friend. I know every rhythm-and-blues station in the country. Most Negro stations are way over on the right on the dial." Ashe does not seem to be quite together unless a radio or a tape recorder is playing. He irritates friends by turning up the music and flipping through books or magazines in the middle of conversations. "I can do three things at once," he explains. His responses to things are interesting, if not always clear. Ideas roll out of him unexamined, and he doesn't seem to care if they collide. He is very bright, fast, and articulate, and sometimes grows impatient with others while they catch up. Of the six young men on the United States Davis Cup Team, he seems to have the widest range of interests. But he often conceals his enthusiasms or commitments, and his all-purpose answer to questions is "Not really."

"Do you care if the sun comes up tomorrow, Arthur?"

"Not really."

He does care, though. He is, for example, acutely anxious about the fate of the astronauts. "They make me so nervous I can't stand it. I'm waiting for our first in-flight fatality. It's like a tennis match—everything is written out, but there are unseen variables that come up." No one could call him—or, apparently, ever has called him—spiteful, mean, or petty. "Arthur Junior is sensitive and observant," Arthur Senior will say. "He's quiet. He's easy go. A lot of people seem to think that he's a little selfish-minded. But when he draws his opinion on you you're marked." He is seldom really loose in white company, but when he is he is full of laughter, and his wit produces more. The disarray of his room notwithstanding, he is thoroughly organized. He keeps a detailed agenda in a huge ledger, which he carries with him wherever he goes. Like his father, he speaks in maxims. "Whenever you hedge, the truth doesn't come out," he might tell someone. "You've got to say it. You must be tactful but truthful." His summary of his own life is that it has been "a succession of fortunate circumstances." He has seen them in perspective. When an Arthur Ashe Day was held in Philadelphia, he said to a friend, "Why are they giving me a day? I'm only a twenty-four-year-old tennis player."

Ashe again threatens Graebner, with an overpowering service return and a scything crosscourt backhand. But Graebner, in the course of things, rocks, hits, and crunches his twelfth ace, right down the middle—a duster, on the chalk. When Ashe realizes how many aces Graebner has hit, he thinks, "Jesus, that's *three games*." Graebner serves. Crunch. The ball skips through the far corner of the service box and slams into the stadium wall. Ace No. 13. Game to Graebner. Games are three–all, third set.

Games pile up like pairs of blocks. In the seventh game, Ashe hits every one of his first serves in. Graebner puts Ashe down in four points in the eighth. Winning the ninth with complete command, Ashe hits an unplayable serve, a clean ace, and two drop shots that die in the grass. One of the drop shots was a drop half volley. "Incredible," Graebner says to himself. "It's just such a hard shot, and he still hasn't missed one—not one, all day." Graebner aces Ashe again, and, in the tenth, beats him four points to nought. Games are five–all. It is a so-called deuce set. Somewhere now the blocks must fall.

New balls are thrown in. Ashe hits a big serve wide to Graebner's forehand, and it is so well placed and powerful that Graebner can't do much more than smother it with his racquet. Graebner can see that Ashe's serve is not likely to weaken, and that he himself is in need of imaginative strategy or he is boxed in. So he plays a planned point—the idea being that he will move according to plan in a kind of surprise attack, winning grandly if Ashe falls in with the plan and losing flagrantly if he does not. He moves in on Ashe's second serve, chips the ball to Ashe's backhand, and—going to the net—runs to the right, planning that Ashe will hit the ball back on the forehand side. Ashe not only does that but hits it in a kind of half lob. There's the ball, a sitter, just hanging there within plucking reach. Graebner delivers a Wagnerian kill. The ball digs a hole in the turf near Ashe's left foot. Ashe is pensive as he walks back to the baseline. "Now, there was Clark playing a planned point. And it worked. I was busy getting down to hit the ball. I didn't see him coming in. I looked up, and he astonished me. He was suddenly there. That's what Rosewall does all the time." Ashe hits a flat serve to Graebner's forehand, and Graebner drives the ball down the line for an outright winner. Fifteen-thirty. Graebner's bid has substance now. He may be winning the set right here. Ashe says to himself, "You can't relax, Arthur. Every point has a hell of a premium on it now." He lifts the ball, whips up his racquet, and cracks a serve into the deep outside corner. Graebner barely touches it. Ashe is thinking, "That was a crucial serve, a crucial serve. If I hadn't won that point right there, I could have been in deep trouble." He hits two more that Graebner can't handle —in all, three straight unplayable serves. Graebner pauses and joins in the crowd's applause, clapping for Ashe, acknowledging what he has done. "He hit it so hard, so fast. There's nothing you can do about that," Graebner tells himself. Game to Ashe. He leads six games to five, third set.

"Figure out your game plan," Ashe tells himself while the two players change ends. "It's five–six. Jesus, you've got to have a plan. He's on the sun side. Lob as much as possible. Keep it away from his forehand. Make no errors."

Graebner's flat serve goes down the middle. Ashe dives for it and blocks it back. Graebner volleys to the backhand corner. Ashe gets to the ball and hits a high defensive lob. It falls behind Graebner, on the baseline. Graebner runs around the high bounce and hits a fadeaway overhead. It catches Ashe unprepared, at the baseline. Ashe feels stupid. He should have been up front. He more or less stops the ball with his racquet at his hip, effecting a kind of drop shot that scarcely gets over the net. Graebner races to it and hits it down the line. Ashe lobs. Graebner looks for the overhead, but he is not quite under the ball when it drops, and he drives it into the net. "That's what stops Clark—his footwork," Ashe thinks. "He didn't really get to it." Love-fifteen.

At this moment, this match, almost over, is as nearly even as any tennis match could be. There is a narrow statistical edge, though, and it is Graebner's. Graebner has won more points on service returns than Ashe has, he has hit more returns safely back than Ashe has, and he has hit more aces. Each has won one set. The present set is in balance. Ashe is ahead by one game. Graebner has the serve. A hundred and eighty-six points have been played by the two players so far. Ashe has won ninety-three. Graebner has won ninety-three. As it happens, the next four points they play will decide it all.

Ashe wipes his forehead with his wristband, licks his lips, crouches low, then dances nervously in place, about a foot behind the baseline, waiting. Graebner rocks back, then forward, lifts the ball, and pounds another good first serve to Ashe's forehand. Ashe blocks it back weakly. Graebner, moving in, picks up the shot with a deep half volley that keeps Ashe on the defensive. Ashe hits a top-spin lob. Graebner lets it drop, gets under the bounce, and chops the ball down the line. Ashe gets to it and hits back a total forehand—the hardest one he has hit all day. Graebner intercepts it at the net and sharply punches a crosscourt volley beyond retrieve. Fifteen-all.

"One or two key hits in a baseball game can break a game open," Ashe will say. "Sometimes I hit two or three shots in a row and break open a match. I'm fairly explosive—in streaks. I hit some great shots. I make some errors, too. Don't be surprised if I *make* some great shots, because I'll try them." Graebner's first serve strikes near the sideline, and Ashe returns it with a reaching forehand. Graebner, in no man's land, drives the ball far into Ashe's backhand corner. Ashe sprints for it, barely gets to it, and sends up a defensive lob. Graebner smashes the overhead straight at Ashe, and Ashe, off his backhand, pounds the ball straight back at Graebner. Graebner volleys hard to Ashe's right. Ashe scrambles again, and hits another defensive lob. Graebner connects with full force on the overhead, driving a heavy ball back to the forehand corner. Ashe reacts so quickly that he has his racquet back and his feet set in time. He is now going to end this point one way or the other. Answering force with force, he blasts a forehand down the line.

Graebner watches, twenty feet away. That point, one of the biggest points of the match and one of the tightest, was also, as it happens, the longest, although the ball crossed the net only ten times. "Wouldn't you know at a moment like that Arthur would tear off an all-time winner," Graebner murmurs to himself. "Arthur's weakness is his forehand. So I play to it on a big point and he hits a great shot." Fifteen-thirty.

Nothing has happened to Graebner's game. It continues at the level of solid excellence that has brought him, all even, to the present crisis. The level of Ashe's game, however, appears to have risen. He is playing with loose, all-out, fluid abandon—prudence be damned. He pushes his glasses into place. Graebner lifts the ball. Crunch. Right down the middle. Ashe swings away and hits a forehand return so hard that Graebner can't handle it. "He's going berserk," Graebner thinks, and the trouble Graebner is in is so deep that he thinks no further. Fifteen-forty. Set point.

Ashe's favorite shot is his backhand—a predilection that sets him apart from most tennis players on all levels. Nineteen years ago, when Ronald Charity began to teach him the game, Charity purposely led him to believe that the backhand was the easiest stroke. "You know how folks are about the backhand—so we practiced that first. It was no trouble getting Arthur to have a *good* backhand. He caught on quickly." In a tight tennis match, a player's forehand is usually the first shot to disintegrate. If his backhand is not strong, he is finished. Dr. Johnson, taking over, had Arthur hit thousands and thousands of backhands, and he said, "If your backhand is your strongest stroke, you'll never break down. Never. It's like putting a man in a briar patch. If he *wants* you to hit to his backhand, he's home free. That's my philosophy. Now hit a hundred more." What developed was a beautiful, rolling stroke, free and open, with more power than most players ever develop in any form. Ashe can underspin it, roll it, hit it flat. He can cradle the ball on his racquet, and hit it with several kinds of timing. He's got it all. He says that his backhand comes in several parts—that it works on a series of pivots, from the shoulders to the elbow to the wrist and the fingers. He has the spring wrist of a Hoad or a Laver, not the strong and rigid wrist of a Graebner or a Trabert, and he thinks that if Graebner could swing the same way Graebner would break the ball open. Tennis players fear Ashe's backhand and say that hitting a second serve to it can be like serving into the mouth of a cannon. Ashe loves the movement of the backhand, because the follow-through does not cramp the arm into the body but does just the opposite—opens both arms wide and high, so that the stroke ends in the stance of the Winged

Victory. He has a remarkable ability to make time seem to stand still for his backhand, because he can delay it somehow, waiting for his opponent to make a move, withholding commitment until the ultimate second, then hitting away. "I like to hit my backhand crosscourt one zillion miles an hour—in. I hit one the other day against Drysdale that gave me consummate pleasure. He was there, but it went by him so fast that he never lifted his racquet. Whee— you fling your arms away from your body and you wind up in a position that looks as if you're calling for help, both arms in the air."

Graebner bounces the ball once, rocks, lifts, and hits a faulted serve. As Graebner prepares to serve again, Ashe is telling himself, "You must *get it in*. Play it safe. If you've got a guy at fifteen-forty, you don't have to try a great shot. All the pressure is on Clark." But Graebner, for some reason, hits his second serve down the middle, toward Ashe's backhand. The temptation is much too much for Ashe, and the shot he hits is by far the greatest of the day. When the ball has left the cannon, Ashe stands on his toes with his arms spread-eagled in the follow-through. The shot is a crosscourt, in-and-out backhand that goes two zillion miles an hour—in. It goes past Graebner so fast that Graebner does not even move. Game to Ashe. He wins the third set, seven–five.

Graebner flings his racquet twenty feet out of the court. Ashe—running toward the portal that leads to the dressing rooms where players rest during the interval between third and fourth sets—drops his racquet on the grass.

"That's a hell of a great way to win a set—blast the ball right by him," Ashe is thinking. "When Graebner comes back on the court, all he'll be able to think about is that backhand and how he couldn't get near it. He gave me my favorite shot. How could he do that?"

And Graebner is thinking, "I didn't know he'd go ape."

There are two identical, adjacent rooms under the grandstands at Forest Hills—long, panelled, wedge-shaped, narrow, each containing a table, a chair, a shower stall, towels, hot tea, Coca-Cola, Gatorade. Graebner throws off his clothes and hurries into a shower, still wearing his glasses. Ashe, on the other side of the wall, sits down and slowly prepares to change his shirt. Graebner rubs soap on his glasses and rinses them. He is thinking, among other things, "One lucky shot here or there makes all the difference in the world."

"The fourth set is for all the ice cream," Ashe is

telling himself. His father is with him. Dr. Johnson comes into the room and reminds Arthur to concentrate, and to be sure, when he returns to the court, to win the first point.

To Ashe and to Graebner this tournament and this match are high and important moments—but passing moments, nonetheless—on the way to Australia. All year, they have played together to get the United States into position for the first time in four years to challenge the Australians, and the concentration of these efforts has resulted in part in a general elevation of each player's game. Ashe, Graebner, Pasarell, Lutz, Smith, Osborne—the United States Davis Cup Team has been a self-improving institution, and had Ashe and Graebner not been on the team it is possible that neither would have come this far at Forest Hills or reached the semifinals at Wimbledon, as both did. In three months' time, they will go to Australia. Ashe and Graebner will play the singles matches, and the team will come home with the Davis Cup. Meanwhile, under the grandstands at Forest Hills, their captain, Donald Dell, has the problem of telling each how to beat the other.

Dell, who is thirty, is an attorney in the District of Columbia. He has sandy hair and he looks like half the older brothers in the world. He was a friend of Senator Robert Kennedy, he worked for a time as a special assistant to Sargent Shriver in the Office of Economic Opportunity, and there is about him a veneer of nice politics, of wheeling and dealing at the compound level. Beneath this veneer is a man of luck, wit, decision, and outspoken fairness, and as man and politician Dell has made a team out of a half-dozen blatantly individual tennis players. The level of his own game could be described as first-rate once removed, so his words have wherewithal. Pasarell is with him. They visit Graebner first. Graebner is putting on fresh clothes.

"Hey, Clark, how you feeling?"

"I just can't beat this guy. I can't beat him. He *always* beats me. I can't play the guy. It's not that I'm psyched out by him, but I'm playing great and he hits three all-time winners in a row. I can't beat him."

"Then take a shower and let's go back to the clubhouse and have a nice beer and default the fourth set. Then you can go home."

"I didn't mean that."

"Don't think like that. Go out there and work your tail off. Don't wake up tomorrow morning regretting that you didn't give a hundred per cent. Win the fourth set and Arthur's morale will go down. You'll have to work your *ass* off. He's playing well now. But you get one break in the fourth set and you're back in the match. Go out there and guts it out. Scramble. When he aces, don't worry. When he hits a wood volley, don't worry about it. Don't worry what people in Cleveland are thinking, watching the tube."

"I'm playing better than Wimbledon."

"Just play Arthur."

"I've been reading him unbelievably well. But when he starts closing his eyes, nobody knows where the ball will go."

Pasarell asks Graebner, "Is there anything I can get you? Anything you need?"

"I need your game for the next hour, Charlie."

Dell says, "Clark, I'm going to see Arthur now. Is there anything you want me to tell him?"

"Yeah. Tell him to turn pro."

Three minutes remain of the interval. Arthur has dried himself off with a towel and changed his shirt, but has made no further effort to cool himself after the infernal heat outside. He doesn't believe in mid-match showers. "They cool you too much, draw too much heat off and sap your energy, even if they *are* refreshing. Back on the court, you've got to use a lot of energy just to get your body working full blast again."

Dell and Pasarell come into the room.

"I'm not serving well," Ashe says.

"Spin it in. And move in faster to the net," Dell tells him.

"I'm not returning well."

"Bend over. Move your feet. Keep your ball on the racquet longer. You're wasting too many shots. You're flailing too many returns. Move your damn feet on the returns. You're gambling too much for winners when it isn't necessary. Play percentage tennis. Hit a three-quarter spin serve and get into the net. He'll chip. Get in there and cover the chip. Arthur, this is the biggest tournament of your life. This is a big chance. The finals are tomorrow. You've got a chance to win the whole thing."

Ashe looks up at Pasarell to see what he might have to say. Pasarell says, "You were asleep in the first set. Wake up."

By the umpire's chair, Graebner unfolds a fresh dental towel, puts it in his pocket, rubs sawdust all over his racquet handle, returns to the court, and slams back Ashe's first two serves of the fourth set. Love-thirty. It is an inaccurately auspicious beginning, for Ashe now begins to hit shots as if God Himself had given them a written guarantee. He plays full, free, windmilling tennis. He hits untouchable forty-five-degree volleys. He hits overheads that skid through no man's land and ricochet off the stadium wall. His backhands win everywhere—crosscourt, down the line—and one of them, a return of a second serve, is almost an exact repetition of the extraordinary shot that finished the third set. "When you're confident, you can do anything," Ashe tells himself. Both he and Graebner are, for the most part, hitting the ball even harder than they have been previously, and the average number of shots per point, which rose slightly in the second and third sets, is down again, to 2.5. Graebner is not in any sense out of the match. His serve seems stronger. His volleys are decisive. Ashe sends a big, flat serve down the middle, and Graebner, standing on the center mark, hits the ball off his forehand so hard that Ashe cannot get near it—an all but impossible shot from that position, requiring phenomenal power. Ashe serves again to Graebner's forehand. Graebner drives another hard return, and runs for the net. Ashe is now playing almost consistently on the level he stepped up to in the last three shots of the third set. Moving fast, he intercepts, and sends a light and graceful putaway past Graebner, down the line.

There are very few places in the world where Ashe feels at ease or at home. One, of course, is Gum Spring, Virginia, where the milieu he moves in is entirely black. His defenses are alert everywhere else he goes, with only four exceptions—Australia, the islands of the South Pacific, Sweden, and Spain. "A Negro draws stares in Australia, but you can pretty much tell they're not malicious. They only mean 'What the hell is *he* doing here?' I don't look like an aborigine. When I first played in Spain, I could tell by the way the Spanish tennis players acted that I had nothing to worry about. The Spaniards would just as soon hustle my sister, if I had one. They don't care. It's a great feeling to get away from all this crap in the United States. Mentally and spiritually, it's like taking a vacation. It's like going from New York to the black world of Richmond and Gum Spring. Your guard goes down. Everywhere else I go, my sensors are out. Everywhere. It's a waste of energy, but maybe I can do two things at one time— think about something else and have my sensors out, too."

In 1960, Arthur was sent to St. Louis for his senior year of high school, and it is generally assumed that this arrangement was made (by Dr. Johnson) because Arthur was not allowed to compete with white tennis players in Richmond. This was true but not relevant. By that time, there was no tennis player of any color in or near Richmond who could play points with him. Tennis is a game of levels, and it is practically impossible for a player who is on one level to play successfully with a player on any other. Arthur needed high-level competition the year around, and St. Louis was full of McKinleys and Buchholzes and indoor courts. There were a few problems. One young St. Louis tennis player took Arthur to a private tennis club one day that spring, and as Arthur was beginning to hit, a voice called out to him, "Hey, you! Get off there. We don't allow colored in this club." Arthur left. He was graduated from Sumner High School with the highest grades in his class. On the summer tennis circuit, he went to every length to attract no attention, to cause no difficulty. Moving in and out of expensive white atmospheres, he used the manners that his father and Dr. Johnson had taught him, and he noticed that the manners of the white players, and much of their general behavior, tended to suggest a lower standard. "When an experience is new, you're not sure of yourself mentally, but basic politeness got me through." Meanwhile, he would look down at his plate and find two steaks there. He knew what was happening. A message had come from the kitchen, on the Afro-American telegraph.

While he was at U.C.L.A., the level of his game became so high that he was made an honorary member of the Beverly Hills Tennis Club, where he played with people like Hank Greenberg and Charlton Heston. Of Heston he says, "He's not that coördinated. He plays tennis like he drives a chariot." Of Greenberg he says, "He's a tennis buff. He covers the court well. He's a big guy. A big, big guy. Jesus!" On a street in the Bronx, Ashe once played tennis with John Lindsay ("Good forehand"), and in the Washington ghetto he played with Bobby Kennedy ("Another good forehand"). In tennis, the nearest black was light-years below him now, and he became, in his own words, "a sociological phenomenon." He has been kept extremely busy on the U-Rent-a-Negro circuit. He has been invited to the White House four times. Only two years ago, he was very hesitant about walking into the dining room of the West Side Tennis Club, in Forest Hills. Sometimes when his phone rings in his rooms at West Point, he picks it up and an anonymous voice says to him, for instance, "You have your nerve running your black ass around the country playing tennis while my son is fighting in Vietnam."

Ashe leads two games to one in the fourth set. He moves in on Graebner's second serve and tries one more backhand crosscourt megablast. Out. By inches. Fifteen-love.

Graebner's next serve is wide to Ashe's backhand. Ashe drives the ball down the line to Graebner's forehand, following to the net. Ashe admits to himself,

"In effect, I'm saying to him, 'O.K., Clark, I can beat you on your forehand.' I'm being a little arrogant." Graebner catches the ball at the limit of his reach and sends back an unforceful volley. Ashe wipes the point away with his backhand. Fifteen-all.

Graebner's big serve goes down the middle. Ashe leaps for it and blocks it back. Graebner hits a low, underspun crosscourt backhand. Ashe runs to it and answers with a backhand even more acutely angled. Graebner has to dive for it, but he gets it, hitting a slow deep volley. Ashe, on the backhand again, drives the ball—much too fast to be contested—down the line. "Get in there!" he shouts, and the ball gets in there. Fifteen-thirty. Graebner thinks, "If I had his backhand and he had my forehand, we'd be invincible."

Ashe's forehand is something to see as it is. Graebner rocks, goes up, and—to Ashe's forehand—smashes the ball. Ashe slams it back through the service box and out the side of the court. "Most players hit a shot like that once in a lifetime," says Donald Dell. Fifteen-forty.

Ashe now has two chances to break Graebner. He looses a heavy backhand return, but Graebner stops it and hits it to the baseline. Ashe lobs. At the service line, Graebner moves in under the overhead and brings down the paper cutter. The shot goes within four feet of Ashe but is too powerful to be as much as touched. Thirty-forty.

Break point No. 2. Graebner rocks, and lifts the ball. Crunch. Unmanageable. Right down the middle. Deuce.

Graebner serves. Fault. Again. Double fault. Advantage Ashe.

Graebner faults once more, then hits a wide slice to Ashe's backhand. Ashe moves to it and explodes another all-time winner down the line. Game to Ashe. Games are three–one, fourth set. Graebner is broken.

Because Ashe is black, many people expect him to be something more than a tennis player—in fact, demand that he be a leader in a general way. The more he wins, the more people look to him for words and acts beyond the court. The black press has criticized him for not doing enough for the cause. He has repeatedly been asked to march and picket, and he has refused. Militant blacks have urged him to resign from the Davis Cup Team. Inevitably, they have called him an Uncle Tom. Once, in Milwaukee, he was asked to march with Stokely Carmichael but said no, and on the same day he visited a number of Milwaukee playgrounds, showing black children and white children how to play tennis. The demands of others have never moved him to do anything out of character. He will say what he thinks, though, if someone asks him. "Intrinsically, I disapprove of what black militants do. Human nature being what it is, I can understand why they have such a strong following. If you had nothing going for you and you were just a black kid in a ghetto, you'd have historical momentum behind you and it would be chic to be a black militant—easy to do, very fashionable. You'd have your picture and name in the paper because you'd be screaming your head off. They sound like fire-and-brimstone preachers in Holy Roller churches. But you must listen to them. You can't completely ignore them. Their appeal is to the here and now. If I were a penniless junkie, I'd go for it, too. I'd have nothing to lose, nowhere to go but up. But you can't change people overnight. If you took a demographic survey of blacks, you'd find, I think, that the farther up the socio-economic scale you got, the fewer people would be behind Stokely. I'm not a marcher. I'm not a sign carrier. I'm a tennis player. If you are a leader in any field, and black, you are a hero to all blacks, and you are expected to be a leader in other fields. It's beautiful. People in Richmond look upon me as a leader whether I like it or not. That's the beautiful part of it. The other side of the coin is that they expect the same of some light-heavyweight boxer that they do of me. But he doesn't have my brain. *He* tries to get into politics, and we lose some leverage.

"Guerrilla warfare is going to start. Businesses will burn. There will be more riots. More nationally known political figures may be killed. But eventually more middle-class blacks will become involved in human rights. Extreme militants will lose their power and influence. So I am cautiously optimistic. I define the cause as the most good for the most people in the least amount of time, and that has absolutely nothing to do, specifically, with color. Anything I can do to help the cause is good. Nobody listens to a loser. If I put myself in a position where I can't compete, I am merely a martyr. We don't need any more martyrs right now. One must separate the emotional from the practical. Don't bite off more than you can chew. A little bit is better than nothing, no matter how you may feel. Progress and improvement do not come in big hunks, they come in little pieces, and the sooner people accept this the better off they'll be. I wouldn't tell my son to content himself that things will come gradually. You've got to push. You've got to act as though you expect it to come tomorrow. But when you know it's not going to come, don't give up. We're outnumbered ten to one. We'll advance by quiet negotiation and slow infiltration—and by objective, well-planned education, not an education in which you're brainwashed. Education reflects a culture's values. If that culture is warped, you get a warped education, with white Janes and Dicks in the schoolbooks and white pale-faced guys who made history. There are so many insidious ways you can get brainwashed to think white equals good—white Howdy-Doody, white Captain Kangaroo. I didn't feel like a crusader once. I do now. I've always been fair with all people. I always wanted to be a solid citizen. I went to college. I graduated. I have put in time in the armed services. I treat all people equally—rich, poor, black, white. I am fairly generous. Nobody can find fault with that. But in the spirit of the times—in some people's eyes —I'm an Uncle Tom. The phrase is empty."

"His racquet is his bag," Ronald Charity's wife, Ruth, says. "Arthur has to fight in his own way." Arthur's sensors are still extremely active. He boils within when he hears a white man call him "boy" or "son." He says, "Do I look like your son?" He also can't stand blacks who tell him not to trust whites, and he says he feels sorry for Negroes who become upset when they see a Negro woman with a white man. At U.C.L.A., he was fond of a white girl, and he saw her with some frequency until her mother saw *him* on TV. He laughs out loud when he tells the story. "It's funny now," he says. "It stung then." He uses "black" and "Negro" interchangeably. In hotels, somewhat inconsistently, he often asks, "Where's the boy for the bags?" He thinks there is a certain inherent motor superiority in black athletes. "At an early age, we seem to be a little looser, a little more athletic than white kids. You go through Harlem and you'll see kids less than five feet tall with pretty good jump shots and hook shots. White kids that age don't have those shots." He is suspicious of Greek standards in art. He wonders where all the other races were when Polyclitus was shaping his canon. He urges white American friends to refresh their perspectives by living in Asia, he pays his annual dues to the National Association for the Advancement of Colored People, and he is not at all troubled by men like Alabama's George Wallace. "Wallace is beautiful. He's doing his own thing. He's actually got a little bit of soul. What I worry about is people who say one thing and do another. Wallace is in his bag, and he enjoys it." Ashe's particular hero is Jackie Robinson—"because of what he went through, the self-control, the perseverance." Asked if he has any white heroes, he says, "Yes, I have. John F. Kennedy, Robert Kennedy, Benjamin Franklin, and Pancho Gonzales."

Tilting forward, looking up, Ashe whips his racquet over the ball and aces Graebner with a sharp-angled serve. "I stood as far over as I possibly could and still he aced me," Graebner mumbles. Ashe misses his next first serve, then follows an American twist recklessly to the net. Graebner chips. Ashe hits the world's most unorthodox volley, on the dead run, drawing his racquet back all the way and smashing the ball out of the air, out of sight, with a full round-house swing. "He just pulls his racquet back and slaps," Clark's father comments, but there is only mild disparagement in the remark, for he adds, "That's what Laver does." (Before the year is out, Laver and Ashe will be ranked first and second in the world.) Ashe hits another wide serve—unmanage-able. Donald Dell says, "Arthur is knocking the hell out of the ball." Graebner thinks, "He's smashing every God-damned first serve, and they're all going in." Ashe leads four games to one, fourth set. His game is so big now that it is beyond containment. There is something about it that suggests a very large aircraft beginning its descent for Kennedy. In Graeb-ner remain sporadic aces.

Twenty-six hours hence, beside the Marquee, Dell, Pasarell, and Graebner will meet spontaneously, from separate parts of the stadium, and go to press-section seats, close to one end of the court. Their teammate will be in the fifth set of the finals, against the Dutch player Tom Okker, and they will help draw him through it—"Move your feet, Arthur." . . . "Bend your knees." . . . "Spin it." . . . "Chip the returns, Arthur." . . . "Get your first serve in." Graebner, Pasarell, and Dell will shout these things in moments when the crowd is clapping, because coaching from the grandstand is not strictly approved. When Ashe breaks through Okker's serve, in the fifth game, he will look up at the Davis Cup group and close his fist, and when the match is over he will turn, point up to them with the handle of his racquet, and bow to them, giving them something of his moment as the winner of the first United States Open Championship. "Subdued disbelief," in his words, is what he will feel, but he will speak with nonchalant clarity into microphones and he will put an arm around his weeping father. When he returns to the United States Military Academy, he will have dinner with the cadet corps, and all the cadets will stand up and cheer for him for three and a half minutes while he pushes his glasses into place and affectionately looks them over.

Meanwhile, he aces Graebner for the last time. Graebner looks at the ball as it goes by, watches it hit the stadium wall, shakes his head, then looks again at the empty air beside him where the ball was and thinks, "I can't believe he can hit it that hard. I didn't even *see* the ball. Arthur is just playing too well. He's forcing me into errors." Games are five–two, fourth set.

Graebner serves to Ashe's forehand. Ashe drives the ball up the middle. Graebner hits hard for Ashe's backhand corner, and misses. Love-fifteen.

Ashe chips a return into the net. Fifteen-all.

Ashe blocks another return into Graebner's forehand service court, and Graebner, rushing in, tries a drop half volley, the extraordinarily difficult shot that has almost been Ashe's signature in this match—that Ashe has scored with time after time. Graebner fails to make it good. He whips himself. "An unbelievable shot for me to try—difficult in the first place, and under this pressure ridiculous. Stupid." Fifteen-thirty.

Graebner now sends his farewell ace past Ashe. Crunch. Right down the middle. Thirty-all.

Graebner rocks, swings, hits. Fault. He lifts the ball again. Double fault. Thirty-forty.

"Match point," Ashe tells himself. "Now I'll definitely play it safe." But Graebner hits the big serve into the net, then hits his second serve to Ashe's backhand. The ball and the match are spinning into perfect range. Ashe's racquet is back. The temptation is just too great, and caution fades. He hits for it all. Game, set, match to Lieutenant Ashe. When the stroke is finished, he is standing on his toes, his arms flung open, wide, and high.